Contents

General Editor's Preface		vii
Acknowledgements		ix
Introduction		1
I	The Early Years	4
II	The Struggle for Power	17
III	Socialism in One Country	31
IV	Government and Repression	45
V	Foreign Policy 1924–1941	59
VI	The Great Patriotic War	74
VII	World War to Cold War	88
VIII	The Final Years	100

D1419836

General Editor's Preface

This book forms part of a series entitled *Documents and Debates*, which is aimed primarily at sixth formers. The earlier volumes in the series each covered approximately one century of history, using material both from original documents and from modern historians. The more recent volumes, however, are designed in response to the changing trends in history examinations at 18 plus, most of which now demand the study of documentary sources and the testing of historical skills. Each volume therefore concentrates on a particular topic within a narrow span of time. It consists of eight sections, each dealing with a major theme in depth, illustrated by extracts drawn from primary sources. The series intends partly to provide experience for those pupils who are required to answer questions on documentary material at A-level, and partly to provide pupils of all abilities with a digestible and interesting collection of source material, which will extend the normal textbook approach.

This book is designed essentially for the pupil's own personal use. The author's introduction will put the period as a whole into perspective, highlighting the central issues, main controversies, available source material and recent developments. Although it is clearly not our intention to replace the traditional textbook, each section will carry its own brief introduction, which will set the documents into context. A wide variety of source material has been used in order to give the pupils the maximum amount of experience – letters, speeches, newspapers, memoirs, diaries, official papers. Acts of Parliament, Minute Books, accounts, local documents, family papers, etc. The questions vary in difficulty, but aim throughout to compel the pupil to think in depth by the use of unfamiliar material. Historical Knowledge and understanding will be tested, as well as basic comprehension. Pupils will also be encouraged by the questions to assess the reliability of evidence, to recognise bias and emotional prejudice, to reconcile conflicting accounts and to extract the essential from the irrelevant. Some questions, *marked with an asterisk*, require knowledge outside the immediate extract and are intended for further research or discussion, based on the pupil's general knowledge of the period. Finally, we hope that students using this material will learn something of the nature of historical inquiry and the role of the historian.

John Wroughton

Acknowledgements

The author and publishers wish to thank the following who have kindly given permission for the use of copyright material:

Curtis Brown Ltd on behalf of the Estate for an extract from *The Unrelenting Struggle* by Winston S. Churchill, 1946, © Estate of Sir Winston Churchill; Collins/Angus & Robertson Publishers for extracts from *Russia from A–Z* by H. A. Freund, 1945; Andre Deutsch Ltd for extracts from *Khruschev Remembers* by N. Khruschev, 1971; The London School of Economics and Political Science for extracts from *Soviet Communism: A New Civilisation*, 1935, Longman, Green & Co; Harcourt Brace Jovanovich Inc for extracts from *Report on the Russians* by W. L. White, © 1945, renewed 1973 by W. L. White; Laurence Pollinger Ltd on behalf of the author for extracts from *Mission to Moscow* by Joseph E. Davies, 1942; Royal Institute of International Affairs for extracts from *Soviet Documents on Foreign Policy*, Vol. III, ed. J. Degras, 1953, Oxford University Press for the Royal Institute of International Affairs; Martin Secker & Warburg Ltd for an extract from *Stalin & Co.* by Walter Durranty, 1949; The University of Michigan Press for extracts from *History of the Russian Revolution* by Leon Trotsky.

Every effort has been made to trace all copyright-holders, but if any have been inadvertently overlooked the publishers will be pleased to make the necessary arrangement at the first opportunity.

Introduction

It is a standard truism that every age writes the history that it requires, so that events long in the past change in significance and importance because of the continuing and changing needs of the present. Few characters in history have seen as many different interpretations, in so short a space of time, as Joseph Stalin. In Russia, it could be said, that as long as he was alive he could do no wrong; and as soon as he died, it seemed he had never done anything right. Outsiders seemed equally contradictory. Distinguished journalists such as Malcolm Muggeridge worshipped Stalin from afar, visited Russia, and then turned completely against communism. Winston Churchill was one of Communist Russia's most bitter opponents and then in World War II became a staunch supporter of Stalin.

One can partly explain these shifting sands of opinion by noting the obvious fact of changing circumstances. People may not have agreed with Stalin but, as long as he was alive, it would be suicidal to let this become known to him. As Churchill himself admitted, it was not that he liked communism, it was just that he disliked Nazism more. Even this cannot explain away the mass of contradictory statements made about Stalin even when he was alive. To take the example of Russian agriculture in the 1930s: some foreign visitors claimed there was a famine, others adamantly protested there was not. Again, one can argue that people may only see what they want to see, to reinforce prejudices already held; but, more importantly, most visitors only saw what the Soviet government wanted them to see. For most of his time in power, Stalin's control was so complete that it was near impossible to discover anything beyond the party line, the official truth. With Stalin's Russia we are not only concerned with motive but often even with such mundane matters as the basic facts; not only with why the purges occurred - whether Stalin killed Kirov, if there was a genuine threat to his leadership - but even their extent: how many were killed? Ambivalence is also seen with the economy, whether the policies of Collectivisation and the Five Year Plans were necessary, whether they were successful, how much hardship they caused, whether this hardship was justified. If the idea that a real plot against Stalin and a genuine fear of foreign invasion merited desperate remedies suggests some consideration of morality, and if the reader, rightly argues that morality has little place in history then, unfortunately, morality muddies the waters still further. Hitler is generally perceived as evil, the Nuremberg Trials as a well deserved reckoning for those Nazis that survived the war. However, at Nuremberg, in the long and sorry list of atrocities, no mention was made of the Katyn Wood massacres. No wonder: all concerned knew it was the Russians who had murdered Polish officers there, but Russia was an ally, and Stalin, of necessity, must be blameless.

Contemporary sources make it no easier to pierce this veil of secrecy. We might expect to find out more about Stalin at the start of his career, when he was not all-powerful: but his background was so humble that this is not easy and his role in the Russian Revolution was scarcely high profile. Once he attained power, the official view is almost unchallenged, and unchallengeable. His Collected Works are numerous, but are largely devoted to endless speeches along with a few minutes from party meetings. They are the official view, no more and no less. Any suggestion of discussion, let alone argument, is entirely absent. We also lack, with very few exceptions, any real view of the informal Stalin, which would be of especial value as the older he got, the fewer meetings he held.

One also searches in vain for opposing views, the memoirs of the important men close to the seat of power. There is a very simple explanation for this. Almost without exception, Stalin had them killed in the great purges. Kamanev, Zinoviev, Bukharin, Rykov, Tomsky: all dead. None dared to leave a written testament for fear it would be found and implicate family and friends. So complete were the purges that those that did survive did so largely because they were of no real consequence: local victims of petty grudges who survived to tell of conditions in the Gulags but certainly had little idea of why they were there.

Such was the fear engendered that little real information escaped. Foreign ambassadors and journalists are often a good source as they are fed government leaks or stories from the opposition; but in Stalin's Russia there was no opposition, and no-one dared leak anything for fear of discovery. The foreign extracts in this book, where they do not reflect the official party line, may cast doubt upon it, but rarely with any concrete proof. Even with the opportunities afforded in World War II, when Allied support meant greater contact with the West, there were few opportunities to find out more. The limits of the extent of our knowledge can be seen by the fact that Trotsky is often cited as a major source of information on Stalin yet he left Russia in the late 1920s, never to return, and retained few contacts with the upper echelons of Soviet power. Even so, he was still judged sufficiently dangerous to merit assassination, on Stalin's orders, in 1940.

One might, at least, expect more honesty from those Soviet politicians who did survive Stalin, those who outlived him. Even here one gets nothing like full honesty. Khrushchev achieved some attention for his Secret Speech but in truth Stalin was largely accused of being somewhat too excessive while his heart was still in the right place. This comes as no surprise when one realises that Khrushchev owed his position to his steadfast application of Stalin's policies, the purges included. Russia's habit of governing via the Old Guard was one that continued well into the 1970s, and thus it did not pay for ex-confederates to complain too strongly about their former senior colleague. One might expect greater openness from the younger leaders, notably Gorbachev, but even here one is disappointed. When communism rarely admits to anything going wrong – although the situation is now changing rapidly – then it would take a major change of policy to admit that one of the main leaders of Communist Russian history got it totally wrong.

This introduction began with the observation that there is no such thing as a stable, unchanging view of history. The present turbulent state of affairs in Russia, the lack of a consensus, makes it even harder to come to an assessment of Stalin. Perhaps recent changes will eventually lead to an opening up of Russian State archives to Western historians. Until that happens, our judgement of Stalin must be partial and flawed.

I The Early Years

Introduction

Even the most hardened critic of Joseph Stalin would find it
difficult to accuse the young Dzhugashvili of opportunism: the
Social Democratic Party in the late 19th century seemed to stand
very little chance of gaining power in the Russia of that time. Based
in Georgia, Stalin, having gone through a number of other aliases
before settling on the 'Man of Steel', acted as a dutiful party
member even to the extent of suffering the obligatory arrest and
internal exile. Unlike his more famous contemporaries, Lenin and
Trotsky, he did not go into extended exile overseas, a fact that
some historians make use of in explaining Stalin's later lack of
interest in international affairs.

He remained in Russia, sided with the Bolsheviks when the party
split in 1903, and steadily rose through the ranks to become a
member of the Central Committee. As a result he was one of the
few senior members of the party present in Russia when revolution
broke out unexpectedly in Petrograd in February 1917. His temporary leadership along with Kamanev was not a profitable one.
The policy the two men adopted, that of lending support to the
provisional government, was one that was immediately repudiated
when Lenin returned to Russia a month later and who in his *April
Theses* demanded 'All power to the Soviets'.

Chastened, Stalin was quick to make his peace with his leader
and to adopt all of Lenin's policies. Indeed so complete was the
change of heart that it became almost impossible to detect any
difference of opinion between the leader and his most loyal disciple.
Stalin's *Collected Works* reveal a paucity of his writings and speeches
from this period and even much later official paintings only reflect
the view that Stalin may have been at every important event in the
summer of 1917 (which was not even true) but always a step behind
Lenin. Stalin's later attempts to inflate his role were mercilessly
attacked by opponents such as Kerensky and Trotsky. He was,
they claimed, not as important as he wished to be seen, not a great
leader but in Sukhanov's memorable phrase merely a 'grey blur'.

It is a telling phrase but perhaps it holds more truth than the
critics intended. Even in the period of the October Revolution and

the Civil War Stalin was building up a power base; and events were to show that if one is gaining power surreptitiously one may not want to flaunt it.

1 Youth

(a) A brief biography

He was born on 21 December 1879 as the son of a shoemaker in the little town of Gori, near Tiflis, Georgia, in the Caucasus. His original name was Dzhugashvili; one of his party aliases was Koba. He attained world fame under his party alias Stalin (The Steel One)
5 said to have been coined by Lenin. He went to the ecclesiastical school at Gori (1888–94) and later to the theological seminary at Tiflis from which he was expelled on 27 May 1899. At that time he had already made himself familiar with the writings of Charles Darwin, Karl Marx and certain of Lenin's works. He became a
10 member of the Georgian section of the Russian Social Democratic Labour Party (RSDLP) where he belonged to the radical left wing. After his expulsion from the seminary Stalin worked pre-eminently in the revolutionary movement of Georgia. Between 1902 and 1913 he was repeatedly arrested by the police and several times sentenced
15 to exile but each time escaped to proceed with his revolutionary activities first in Batum and Baku, later in St Petersburg. From the formation of the Bolshevik wing of the RSDLP at the second Party Congress 1903 Stalin, then in Eastern Siberian exile, sided with Lenin's Bolsheviks. He attended the Tammerfors (Finland) Confer-
20 ence of the Bolsheviks (December 1905) where he first met Lenin, and participated in the third (1905) and fourth (1906) Party Congresses. At the Prague Conference of the Party (January 1912) Stalin was elected in his absence a member of the Central Committee for organising revolutionary work within Russia. He visited
25 Lenin in Cracow in November 1912 and took part at the August 1913 Conference of the Central Committee at Poronino.

> Freund, H. A. (1945) *Russia from A to Z* (Sydney: Angus Robertson Ltd) p. 523.

(b) From student to revolutionary

A glance at the memoirs of his contemporaries, some of them written long before he reached his present greatness, bears witness that even at this early stage there was a peculiarly decisive and
30 unalterable quality about the way in which Stalin entered the political arena arguing a sense of destiny unusual in a youth. One of his school friends in a small volume of memoirs published about 1924 recalls the picture of young Stalin riding on the shoulders of a

comrade crying in his rather harsh voice 'Ja Stal' – I am Steel.
35 Whether the incident is apocryphal or not is beside the point; it
serves to illustrate the fact that Stalin was very early conscious of
his power and his future calling.

By the time he reached the age of eighteen his growing reputation at the Seminary brought him under the watchful eye of
40 Jordania and the Georgian Social Democrats. Under their guidance
Stalin began to read with increasing voracity the forbidden books
of European Marxism; as he himself rather naively described it
many years later to Henri Barbusse: 'I joined the Revolutionary
movement at the age of fifteen when I found myself in sympathy
45 with the secret groups of Russian Marxists existing in Trans-
caucasia. These groups exercised a strong influence over me and
gave me a taste for clandestine literature'.

Such activities in a High School staffed by reactionary professors
and controlled by the Orthodox Church could not continue
50 indefinitely. It appears that Stalin was first warned quietly by the
Rector that his conduct was unsatisfactory and might lead to
trouble but in spite of his extreme youth he was already irrevocably
dedicated to his chosen career. He accepted the warning without
comment – and went back to his pamphlets and his work. By 1899,
55 at the age of nineteen, the reputation of Sosso Dzugasgvili had
grown sufficiently to cause the Tiflis police to take an interest in his
activities among the factory and railway workers of the city.
Reports were received by the Seminary authorities describing their
pupil's part in several strikes at which Stalin was frequently seen
60 distributing the literature of the Georgian Social Democratic
group. This provided the last straw. An immediate search was
instituted of Stalin's room at the Seminary as a result of which were
found according to the official comment 'books on the natural
sciences, sociology and the working-class movement together with
65 numerous leaflets and other propagandist material'.

Whatever the reason, in 1899 Stalin ceased to attend the Seminary. Without a moment's hesitation, without seeking to justify
himself to the outer world into which he was so suddenly thrown,
he went, in the graphic words of a friend, 'straight over to the
70 workers without a backward glance'. Russian Social Democracy
had gained one of its ablest recruits since Lenin.

So ended the first period of Stalin's life, leaving him with his feet
firmly planted on the revolutionary road, a road beset with dangers
and offering no reward except the certainty of exile, imprisonment
75 and worse. From this time Stalin ceased to be a Georgian and
became in increasing degree a Russian; but though he succeeded in
rising above the limited outlook of a backward and provincial
people he carried with him and still carries the imprint of his
birthplace revealing it at every major crisis of his life. Georgia has
80 given to Stalin his ruthlessness, his quality of steel; he possesses his

country's patience and ability to endure in silence yet never to forget. Like Georgia, Stalin can resist without seeming to fight, he can wait in apparent impotence only to seize with uncanny instinct upon the most propitious moment to take action.

Cole, D. M. (1942) *Joseph Stalin, Man of Steel* (London: Rich and Cowan) pp. 12–13.

Questions

a According to extract (*a*) what were Stalin's links with Lenin?
b Does extract (*a*) give the impression that Stalin was an important Bolshevik in the period before 1914?
★ c What sources are used to put together the account in extract (*a*) and how trustworthy are they?
d Why did Stalin leave the Seminary according to extract (*b*)?
e Is extract (*b*) in favour of Stalin?

2 The provisional government

(a) An opponent's view

Not long before Lenin's arrival in Petrograd an article by none other than Joseph Stalin appeared in *Pravda* on March 15 1917 shortly after his return from exile:

'The war goes on. The great Russian Revolution has failed to put
5 an end to it and there is no hope that it will end tomorrow or the day after. The soldiers, peasants and workers of Russia who went to war at the call of the deposed Tsar, and who shed their blood under his banners, have freed themselves and the Tsarist idols have been replaced by the red banners of the Revolution. But the war
10 will continue because the German troops have not followed the example set by the Russian Army and are still obeying their Emperor who avidly seeks his prey on the battlefield of death.

When one army confronts another, the most absurd policy would be to propose that one of them lays down their arms and
15 goes home. This policy would not be a policy of peace but a policy of slavery, a policy that free people would reject with indignation. No, the free people will stand firmly at their posts, will reply bullet with bullet, shell with shell. This is inevitable.

The revolutionary soldiers and officers who have overthrown
20 the yoke of tsarism will not leave the trenches so as to make room for the German or Austrian soldiers and their officers who as yet have not had the courage to free themselves from the yoke of their governments. We cannot permit any disorganisation of the military forces of the Revolution. War must be ended in an orderly way by a

25   pact among the liberated peoples and not by subordination to the
will of the imperialist conqueror.'

        Kerensky, Alexander (1966) *The Kerensky Memoirs* (London:
        Cassell) p. 261.

(b) Trotsky's opinion

    Kamanev, a member of the·emigrant editorial staff of the central
organ, Stalin, a member of the Central Committee and Muranov, a
deputy in the Duma who had also returned from Siberia, removed
30   the old editors of *Pravda*, who had occupied a too 'left' position and
on 15th of March, relying on their somewhat problematical rights,
took the paper into their own hands. In the programme announcement of the new editorship it was declared that the Bolsheviks
would decisively support the provisional government 'in so far as
35   it struggles against reaction or counter-revolution'. The new
editors expressed themselves no less categorically upon the question of war: while the German army obeys its Emperor the Russian
soldier must 'stand firmly at his post answering bullet with bullet,
shell with shell.' 'Our slogan is not the meaningless "down with
40   war". Our slogan is pressure upon the provisional government
with the aim of compelling it to make an attempt to induce all the
warring countries to open immediate negotiations, and until then
every fighting man remains at his post!' Both the idea and its
formulation are the work of the defencists. This programme of
45   pressure upon an imperialist government with the aim of 'inducing'
it to adopt a peace-loving form of activity was the programme of
Kautsky in Germany, Jean Longuet in France, MacDonald in
England. It was anything but the programme of Lenin who was
calling for the overthrow of imperialist rule. Defending itself
50   against the patriotic press *Pravda* went even farther: 'All "defeat-
ism"', it said, 'or rather what an undiscriminating press protected
by the tsar's censorship has branded with that name died at the
moment when the first revolutionary regiment appeared on the
streets of Petrograd'. This was a direct abandonment of Lenin.

        Trotsky, Leon (1980) *The History of the Russian Revolution*
        (New York: Monad Press) p. 290.

(c) Stalin's explanation

55   To Lenin's old guard it seemed their master had gone mad. His
platform was so alien to the prevailing mood in the high party
circles that the *Pravda* publishing Lenin's famous *April Theses*
embodying his stand attached to it a note expressing the editors' –
of whom Stalin was one – disagreement with their chief. Yet it is
60   this catechism that forms today the cornerstone of Stalin's doctrine
of power.

Lenin went over the heads of his associates and appealed directly to the masses. At the same time he reached out for an alliance with the independent group led by Trotsky. He launched a campaign
65 against the 'old Bolsheviks who more than once played a sorry part in the history of our party by repeating a formula unintelligently learned instead of studying the peculiar nature of the new and living reality'.

'Kamanev and Rykov tried to resist', writes Trotsky. 'Stalin
70 silently stepped aside. Not one of his articles written about this period shows that Stalin made any attempt to estimate his previous policy and win his way back to Lenin's stand. He simply kept silent because he had been too much compromised by his unfortunate leadership during the first months of the revolution. He preferred
75 to withdraw into the background. He never made any public appearance to defend Lenin's views; he merely stood back and waited.'

Stalin never denied his vacillations. The strength of his defence lies in the fact he shared his views with many of the party leaders
80 and that he never pretended to be the originator of policies or the infallible leader that Trotsky would make himself. 'It's no wonder that the Bolsheviks, having been scattered by Tsarism in prison and exile, and only now able to come together from all the ends of Russia to work out a new platform could not in one stroke find
85 their way in the new situation. I shared my mistaken viewpoint with the majority of the party and surrendered it fully about the middle of April adopting Lenin's *April Theses*.' Such was Stalin's apology years later.

> Levine, Isaac (1931) *Stalin, A Biography* (London: Jonathan Cape) p. 104.

Questions

a What views on the war are expressed by Stalin in extract (*a*)?
b Why did Kerensky refer to an article by 'none other than Joseph Stalin' (lines 1–2) in this extract?
c Compare extracts (*a*) and (*b*). What implicit criticisms of Stalin are made and how are they put over?
★ d Why might both Kerensky and Trotsky dislike Stalin?
e According to extract (*c*) how did Stalin explain away his difference of opinion with Lenin?

(d) The grey blur

At this time Stalin appeared in the Ex Comm. for the Bolsheviks, in addition to Kamanev. This man was one of the central figures of the Bolshevik Party and perhaps one of the few individuals who

5   held (and hold to this day) the fate of the revolution and of the State in their hands. Why this is so I shall not undertake to say: 'influence' in these exalted and irresponsible spheres remote from the people and alien to publicity is so capricious. But at any rate Stalin's role is bound to be perplexing. The Bolshevik Party in spite of the low level of its 'officers' corp had a whole series of most massive figures

10   and able leaders among its 'generals'. Stalin however during his modest activity in the Ex Comm. produced – and not only on me – the impression of a grey blur looming up now and then dimly and not leaving any trace. There is really nothing more to be said about him.

> Sukhanov, N. N. (1983) *The Russian Revolution 1917: A Personal Record* (Princeton: Princeton University Press) p. 230.

(e) Stalin and Lenin

15   In the first week of May an all-Russian Bolshevik conference was héld in Petrograd. Here Stalin came out in favour of Lenin's resolution. From that moment on he remained faithful to his master, a loyal fellow-conspirator. Later in the summer the Bolshevik Party, after a lapse of ten years, once more elected a

20   Central Committee. Stalin was one of its members. For the first time the Central Committee formed the all-powerful Political Bureau. Stalin was on it. This bureau was fated to play a transcendental part in the evolution of the dictatorship and the career of Stalin in the next decade. The Central Committee was in charge of

25   three secretaries, Stalin was one of them. The official organ of the party had an editorial council, Stalin remained one of the editors. He was one of the founders of Bolshevik publishing enterprises and presses. When the Soviet insurrection was in the process of being hatched, an organisational Committee of Seven and a Political

30   Committee of Five under Trotsky were appointed to consummate it. Stalin was a member of both.

There were many breaks and conflicts within the party during the following months. Sharp issues developed between Lenin and various groups of his followers. Stalin never shared in them. He

35   either consciously abnegated all claim to independent thought and sincerely attaching himself to Lenin as a lieutenant in action, or he consciously chose to bide his time to let others wrangle and fight and wear themselves out so as to enable him to emerge at the proper moment with an unimpaired if colourless political record.

> Levine, *op. cit.*, p. 105

Questions

a   In what ways is extract (*d*) biased against both the Bolsheviks in general and Stalin in particular?

b According to extract (*e*) how did Stalin build up power for himself?

c Compare extracts (*d*) and (*e*) in their assessments of Stalin's powers and role in the Bolshevik party in the summer of 1917.

3 The October Revolution

(a) Stalin and the revolution

In the room of the Military Revolutionary Committee were members of the Central Committee of the Bolshevik Party. Lenin and Stalin took a most active and decisive part in all the details of the Military Revolution Committee.

5   At Lenin's suggestion, a Revolutionary Staff was formed under Stalin's direct leadership, which drew up the plans of the operation and distributed the forces. Special units were told to seize the most important centres.

Stalin supervised the carrying out of Lenin's orders. He received
10   delegations from the factories and summoned and carefully instructed the district Party organisers. He performed prodigious work in preparing the garrison to resist the forces of Krasnov and Kerensky. Scores of Commissars as well as rank-and-file soldiers came to him to report on the temper of the men.

Gorky, M. and Stalin, J. (ed.) (1935) *A History of the Civil War in the USSR* (Moscow) p. 25.

(b) Another version

15   Stalin, generally speaking, did not turn up at Smolny. The more decisive the pressure of the revolutionary masses became, and the greater the scope assumed by events, the more Stalin would keep in the background, the paler would become his political thought, the weaker his initiative. . . . When it became clear that the publication
20   of the minutes of the Central Committee for 1917 only laid bare an October gap in the biography of Stalin, the bureaucratic historians created the legend of the 'practical centre'. An explanation of this story – widely popularised during these last years – becomes a necessary element of any critical history of the October revolution.
25   At the conference of the Central Committee in Lesny on the 16th of October one of the arguments against forcing the insurrection was to point out that 'we have not yet even a centre'. At Lenin's suggestion, the Central Committee decided straightaway at that hasty meeting in a back corner to make good the lack. The minutes
30   read: 'The Central Committee organises a military revolutionary centre consisting of the following members: Sverdlov, Stalin, Bubnov, Uritsky, and Dzerzhinsky. This centre becomes a consti-

tuent part of the revolutionary Soviet committee'. This revolution
which everyone had forgotten was first discovered in the archives
in 1924. It began to be quoted as a most important document. Thus
Yaroslavasky wrote: 'This organ (and no other) guided all the
organisations which took part in the insurrection (the revolutionary
military units – the Red Guards)'. These words 'and no other'
reveal frankly enough the goal of this whole *ex post facto* construction. But Stalin has written still more frankly: 'In the staff of the
practical centre summoned to lead the insurrection Trotsky strangely
enough ... was not included'. In order to be in a position to
develop this idea, Stalin was compelled to omit the second half of
the resolution: 'This centre becomes a constituent part of the
revolutionary Soviet committee'. If you bear in mind that the
Military Revolutionary Committee was headed by Trotsky, it is
not hard to understand why the Central Committee was content
with naming the new workers who were to help those already
standing in the centre of the work. Neither Stalin nor Yaroslavsky
has ever explained moreover why the 'practical centre' was first
remembered in 1924.

Between the 16th and 20th of October the insurrection conclu-
sively took the Soviet road. The Military Revolutionary Committee, from the moment of its birth, had the direct leadership not only
of the garrison but of the Red Guard which from October 13th on
was subject to the Petrograd Executive Committee. No place
remained for any other directing centre. Neither in the minutes of
the Central Committee nor in any other material whatever relating
to the second half of October can you discover the slightest trace of
the activity of this supposedly so important institution. Nobody
makes a report of its labours; no tasks are allotted to it; its very
name is never pronounced by anyone although its members are
present at sessions of the Central Committee and take part in the
decision of questions which ought to come directly within the
competence of a 'practical centre'.

Trotsky, *op. cit.*, pp. 368–9

Questions

a Compare extracts (**a**) and (**b**) on the role of the Military
   Revolutionary Committee.
b Compare these extracts on the role of the Revolutionary Staff/
   Revolutionary Centre.
c According to extract (**b**), how and why did Stalin falsify the
   story of the October Revolution?
d What do these sources indicate about the characters of Stalin and
   Trotsky?

(c) Support for a revolution

The day for the uprising must be properly chosen. It is only in this sense that the resolution must be understood. We must wait for the government to attack, it is said. But let us be clear what attack means. When bread prices are raised, when Cossacks are dispatched
5 to the Donets area, etc., that is already an attack. How long should we wait if there is no military attack? Objectively what Kamanev and Zinoviev propose would enable the counter-attack to prepare and organise. We would be retreating without end and would lose the revolution. Why should we not ensure for ourselves the
10 possibility of choosing the day and the conditions for the uprising, so as to deprive the counter-revolution of the possibility of organising?

Comrade Stalin then proposed to analyse the international situation, and argued that there must be more confidence. There are two
15 policies: one is heading towards the victory of the revolution and looks to Europe; the other has no faith in the revolution and counts on only being an opposition. The Petrograd Soviet has already taken the path of insurrection by refusing to sanction the withdrawal of the troops. The navy has already risen in so far as it has
20 gone against Kerensky. Hence we must firmly and irrevocably take the path of insurrection.

> Speech at the meeting of the Central Committee October 16 1917, reprinted in: J. V. Stalin (1953) *Works* vol. 3, (New York: Laurence and Wishart Ltd) p. 8

(d) Stalin the manipulator

During the last week before the insurrection Stalin was obviously manouevering between Lenin, Trotsky and Sverdlov on the one hand, and Kamanev and Zinoviev on the other. In questions of
25 intra-party manouevering he was a past master. Just as in April, after Lenin's arrival, Stalin cautiously pushed Kamanev forward and himself waited on the sidelines in silence before again joining battle, so now on the eve of the insurrection he was obviously making ready in case of possible failure a retreat along the Kamanev
30 and Zinoviev line. Stalin moved along that road up to the limit beyond which it would have entailed a break with the majority of the Central Committee. That prospect frightened him. At the session of the 21st Stalin repaired his half-destroyed bridge to the left wing of the Central Committee by moving that Lenin prepare
35 the theses upon fundamental questions for the Congress of Soviets and that Trotsky make the political report. Both these motions were unanimously adopted. Having thus insured himself on the left, Stalin, at the last moment, withdrew into the shadows: he would wait. All the newest historians, beginning with Yaroslavsky,

40 carefully steer around the fact that Stalin was not present at the
session of the Central Committee in Smolny on the 24th, and did
not take upon himself any function in the organisation of the
insurrection. Nevertheless this fact, indisputably established by the
documents, characterises better than anything else the political
45 personality of Stalin and his methods.

Trotsky, *op. cit.* p. 367.

Questions

a Why might extract (**c**) have been reprinted in Stalin's collected
works many years later?

b How does the account of Stalin's actions in extract (**d**) contra-
dict his speech given in extract (**c**)?

c What impression of Stalin is given by extract (**d**)?

★ d What part did Stalin play in the October Revolution?

4 Trotsky and the Civil War

(a) Trotsky on his own importance

After the October Revolution I was in office for about nine years. I
took a direct part in the building of the Soviet state, revolutionary
diplomacy, the Red Army, economic organisation and the Communist International. For three years, I directly led the Civil War.
5 In this harsh work I was forced to resort to drastic measures. For
these I bear full responsibility before the world working class and
before history. The justification of rigorous measures lay in their
historical necessity and progressive character, in their correspondence with the fundamental interest of the working class. To all
10 repressive measures dictated by the conditions of civil war I gave
their real designation and I have given a public accounting of them
before the working masses. I had nothing to hide from the people
as today I have nothing to hide from the Commission.

When in certain circles of the Party, not without the behind-the-
15 scenes participation of Stalin, opposition arose to my methods of
directing the Civil War, Lenin, in July, 1919, on his own initiative,
and in a fashion wholly unexpected by me, handed me a sheet of
blank paper on the bottom of which he had written: 'Comrades,
knowing the harsh character of Comrade Trotsky's orders, I am
20 convinced, so asbolutely convinced, of the rightness expediency
and necessity, for the good of our cause of the orders he has given,
that I give them my full support'.

There is no date on the paper. In case of need, the date was to be
inserted by myself. Lenin's caution in everything that concerned his
25 relations to the workers is known. Nevertheless he considered it
possible to countersign in advance an order coming from me even

though on these orders often depended the fate of great numbers of men. Lenin did not fear that I would abuse my power.

'The Case of Leon Trotsky', *Report on Hearings of the charges made against him in the Moscow Trials*, (1937) (Secker and Warburg) p. 473.

(b) A supporter of Stalin

In the period 1918 to 1920 Stalin was probably the only person
30 whom the Central Committee shifted about from front to front, selecting the most vulnerable spots, the places where the threat to the revolution was most imminent. Stalin was never to be found where things were comparatively quiet, where success was attend-ing our arms. But wherever, for various reasons, the Red Army
35 suffered reverses, wherever the counter-revolutionary forces, pressing their successes, threatened the very existence of Soviet power, wherever alarm and panic might at any moment develop into helplessness and catastrophe – there Comrade Stalin was always sure to appear. During endless nights, forgoing sleep, he
40 organised things, took the reins of leadership into his own firm hands, and ruthlessly broke down all obstructions.

At the beginning of June 1918, Comrade Stalin, together with a company of Red Army men and two armoured cars, left for Tsaritsyn, in the capacity of Commissar-General for food supplies
45 in South Russia. In Tsaritsyn he encountered incredible chaos. Comrade Stalin reacted with tremendous energy and in a short time from Commissar-General for food supplies he became the active leader of all the Red forces on the Tsaritsyn front.

Voroshilov, K. (n.d.) *Stalin and the Red Army* (Moscow: Foreign languages) p. 24

(c) Stalin to Lenin

Comrade Lenin, just a few words.
50 (1) If Trotsky is going to hand out credentials right and left without thinking – to Trifonev (Don region), to Avtonomov (Kuban region), to Koppe (Stavropol), to members of the French mission (who deserve to be arrested) etc. – it may be safely said that within a month everything in the North Caucasus here will go to pieces
55 and we shall lose the region altogether. Trotsky is behaving in the way Antonov did at one time. Knock it into his head that he must make no appointments without the knowledge of the local people, otherwise the result will be to discredit the Soviet power.

Letter from Stalin to Lenin from Tsaritsyn July 10 1918, reprinted in: J. V. Stalin, *Works*, vol. 4, p. 210.

Questions

a According to extract (**a**) what criticisms were levelled against Trotsky and how did he excuse them?

b What is the purpose of Trotsky's references to Lenin in this extract?

c What role did Stalin play in the civil war, according to extract (**b**)?

d Compare extracts (**a**) and (**b**) on the positive achievements of Trotsky and Stalin.

e What criticisms are made of Trotsky in extract (**c**)?

★ f Who emerged with the greater credit at the end of the civil war, Trotsky or Stalin?

II The Struggle for Power

Introduction

Lenin's premature death in early 1924 precipitated an unedifying scramble for power among his leading lieutenants. In one sense this might be deemed irrelevant. There was no post of 'leader' as such: Lenin had dominated proceedings by sheer dint of personality. The fact that he could so easily dominate Stalin, Zinoviev, Kamanev and even Trotsky said little for the potential leadership powers of these men. Lenin's Testament can be seen therefore not as a list of preferences as to who should replace him, but more a general overview of a group of men destined to share power on Lenin's demise.

None of the four above-mentioned escaped criticism in the Testament; thus all chose to ignore or belittle its importance as the leadership struggle began in earnest. The fight, which occupied much of the mid-1920s, was in part personal diatribe clumsily mixed in with criticism of individuals' purity of communist interpretation. Trotsky, the most notable lieutenant, in fact proved an easy target. Brilliant but arrogant, he had always depended upon Lenin for protection. Judicious quotes from his pre-Bolshevik attacks on Lenin did him little good and further selective quotes from Lenin 'revealed' that Trotsky's foreign policy approach of Permanent Revolution was wrong while Stalin's Socialism in One Country was right.

Zinoviev and Kamanev were similarly outmanouevered. For too long they continued to support the peasants who were reaping the benefits of the New Economic Policy, at the expense of the workers. They too fell from power. The last major grouping, that led by Bukharin, supported the peasants even longer and consequently stood even less chance of success.

Yet in a sense all the arguments over policy were irrelevant. Stalin triumphed by careful use of his position as Party Secretary. He packed the Soviets with his supporters and it was on his instructions that they voted down Stalin's opponents. So complete was Stalin's control that he even got the party to vote against 'faction' and effectively silenced Trotksy, Zinoviev and Kamanev after they had lost their chief posts. Stalin did not just defeat the opposition; henceforth he made it illegal.

1 Lenin's Testament

(a) The Testament

Comrade Stalin having become General Secretary has concentrated an enormous power in his hands; and I am not sure that he always knows how to use that power with sufficient caution. On the other hand, Comrade Trotsky is distinguished not only by his excep-
5 tional abilities – personally he is to be sure the most able man in the present Central Committee – but also by his too far-reaching self-confidence and a disposition to be too much attracted by the purely administrative side of affairs. These two qualities of the two most able leaders of the Central Committee might quite innocently lead
10 to a split; if our party does not take measures to prevent it a split might arise unexpectedly.

I will not characterise the other members of the Central Committee as to their personal qualities. I will only remind you that the October episode of Zinoviev and Kamanev was not of course
15 accidental, but that it ought as little to be used against them personally as the non-Bolshevism of Trotsky.

Bukharin is not only the most valuable and biggest theoretician of the party, but may legitimately be considered the favourite of the whole party; but his theoretical views can only with the very
20 greatest doubt be regards as fully marxist. Of course both these remarks are made by me merely with a view to the present time or supposing that these two able and loyal workers may not find an occasion to supplement their knowledge and correct their onesideness.
25 Postscript: Stalin is too rude, and this fault entirely supportable in relations amongst us Communists becomes insupportable in the office of General Secretary. Therefore, I propose to the comrades to find a way to remove Stalin from that position and to appoint it to another man who, in all respects, differs from Stalin only in
30 seniority – namely more patient, more loyal, more polite and more attentive to comrades.

> Quoted in: S. Hendel (1959) *The Soviet Crucible* (New York: Van Nostrand) p. 281.

(b) A Commentary

In the last few weeks of 1922, Lenin completed the letter to the Party which is now generally known as the 'Lenin Testament'. The name conveys a wrong impression; it was in no sense a will, for
35 Lenin never regarded his position as something to be bequeathed to another; he knew that he occupied the President's chair because of his abilities alone; it was his dearest wish that his successor should do likewise.

How wrong he was, how tragically optimistic, can be clearly

40 seen from the fate of the Testament itself. The Party leaders, each
of whom knew its contents, first decided not to publish it while its
author was alive and later postponed publication indefinitely.
Trotsky, who was later to make much of the 'Testament', concur-
red in this decision which was broken finally by accident. A copy
45 had been received by a visitor to the USSR, the American left-wing
journalist Max Eastman, who promptly gave it worldwide publicity
in the press of the United States. Sad reflection that the last words
of so great a leader should reach the Russian people from a back-
stage newspaper scoop in New York.
50   In the Testament Lenin gave a brief characterisation of the
leading figures of the Party. Trotsky, brilliant but too diverse in his
interests; Zinoviev and Kamanev, indecisive and untrustworthy in
a crisis; Bukharin, clever but not a confirmed Marxist; Stalin also
received his share of criticism as being 'too rude' to fill the office of
55 General Secretary to everyone's satisfaction. In spite of this, Lenin's
rebuke to Stalin is the least severe of all; the faults of the others lay
in fundamental weaknesses. Stalin was simply too brusque to
smooth over the trivial personal frictions of his subordinates.
    Stalin himself has always regarded Lenin's reference to him as
60 more of a compliment than otherwise. In an address to a later
Congress he repeated the words adding 'Yes Comrades I am rude
to those who seek to weaken the Party by their activities and I shall
continue to be rude to such people'.
        Cole, *op. cit.* p. 60

(c) Khrushchev on the Testament

Only in this connection does the full meaning of the so-called 'Will'
65 become clear. Lenin names only six people there and sums them up
briefly, weighing each word. Unquestionably, his object in making
the will was to facilitate the work of direction for me. He naturally
wanted to do it with the least possible amount of friction. He talks
about everyone most guardedly, softening the most devastating
70 judgements. At the same time he qualifies with reservations the too
definite indication of the one whom he thinks entitled to first place.
Only in his analysis of Stalin does one feel a different tone, a tone
which in the later postscript to the will is nothing short of
annihilating.
75   Of Zinoviev and Kamanev Lenin writes with an effect of
casualness, that their capitulation in 1917 was not an accident; in
other words it is in their blood. Obviously such men cannot direct
the revolution but they should not be reproached for their pasts.
Bukharin is not a Marxist but a scholastic; he is however a
80 sympathetic person. Pyatakov is an able administrator but a very
bad politician. It is quite possible, however, that these two,
Bukharin and Pyatakov, will still learn. The ablest is Trotsky; his

defect is his excess of self-confidence. Stalin is rude, disloyal, and capable of abuse of the power that he derives from the party
85 apparatus. Stalin should be removed to avoid a split. This is the substance of the will. It rounds out and clarifies the proposal that Lenin made to me in our last conversation.

Lenin came to know Stalin really only after the October revolution. He valued his firmness and his practical mind which is three-
90 quarters cunning. And yet at every step Lenin struck at Stalin's ignorance, at his very narrow political horizon and his exceptional moral coarseness and unscrupulousness. Stalin was elected to the post of general secretary to the party against the will of Lenin who acquiesced only so long as he himself headed the party. But after his
95 first stroke when he returned to work with his health undermined, Lenin applied himself to the entire problem of leadership. This accounts for the conversation with me. Hence, too, the will. Its last lines were written on 4 January. After that, two more months passed, during which the situation took definite shape. Lenin was
100 now preparing not only to remove Stalin from the post of general secretary but to disqualify him before the party as well. On the question of monopoly of foreign trade, on the national question, on questions of the regime in the party, of the worker-peasant inspection, and of the commission of control, he was systematically
105 preparing to deliver at the Twelfth Congress a crushing blow at Stalin as personifying bureaucracy, the mutual shielding among officials arbitrary rule, and general rudeness.

Quoted in: N. Khrushchev (1971) *Khrushchev Remembers* (London: Andre Deutsch) pp. 499–500.

Questions

a Who receives the most positive appraisal in extract (**a**)?
★ b What is the 'October episode' referred to in line 14?
★ c Why was the postscript (lines 25–31) added later?
d Is the summary of Lenin's Testament in extract (**b**) an accurate one?
e According to extract (**b**), what was the aim of the Testament and why was this not achieved?
f Compare the summaries of the Testament given in extracts (**b**) and (**c**).
g According to extract (**c**), why was Lenin latterly opposed to Stalin?
★ h Why did Lenin not carry out the threats to demote Stalin as stated in extract (**c**)?

2 Permanent Revolution?

(a) Stalin attacks Trotsky

Comrade Stalin considers that if we accept the slogan of a revolutionary war we shall be playing into the hands of imperialism. Trotsky's position cannot be called a position at all. There is no revolutionary movement in the West, there is no evidence of a
5 revolutionary movement. It exists only in potential and in our practical activities we cannot rely merely on potentials. If the Germans begin to advance it will strengthen the hands of the counter-revolution here at home. Germany can advance because she has her own Kornilov troops – her 'Guards'. In October we
10 talked of a sacred war against imperialism because we were told the mere word 'peace' would be enough to start a revolution in the West. But that has not proved correct. Our socialist reforms are stirring up the West but wee need time to carry them out. If we accept Trotsky's policy, we shall create the worst possible condi-
15 tions for a revolutionary movement in the West. Comrade Stalin, therefore, recommends the adoption on Comrade Lenin's proposal for the conclusion of peace with the Germans.

> Speech at the Central Committee January 11, 1918, reprinted in: J. V. Stalin *Works* vol. 4, p. 220

(b) A further attack

Some of those who took part in the October Revolution were convinced that the socialist revolution in Russia could be crowned
20 with success and that this success could be lasting only if the revolution in Russia were directly followed by the outbreak of a more profound and serious revolutionary explosion in the West which would support the revolution in Russia and impel it forwards, it being, moreover, taken for granted that such an explosion
25 was bound to break out. That view has been refuted by events since socialist Russia, which did not receive direct revolutionary support from the Western proletariat, and is surrounded by hostile states, has successfully continued to exist and develop for 3 years already.

> Speech of October 27, 1920 reprinted in: J. V. Stalin *Works* vol. 4, p. 391

(c) Interpreting Lenin

Lenin speaks of the alliance between the proletariat and the
30 labouring strata of the peasantry as the basis of the dictatorship of the proletariat. Trotsky sees a 'hostile collision' between the 'proletarian vanguard' and the 'broad masses of the peasantry'.

Lenin speaks of the leadership of the toiling and exploited masses by the proletariat. Trotsky sees 'contradictions in the position of a

35 workers' government in a backward country with an overwhelmingly peasant population'.

According to Lenin, the revolution draws its strength primarily from among the workers and peasants of Russia itself. According to Trotsky, the necessary strength can be found only 'in the arena
40 of the world proletarian revolution'.

But what if the world revolution is fated to arrive with some delay? Is there any ray of hope for our revolution? Trotsky offers no ray of hope for 'the contradictions in the position of a workers' government could be solved only . . . in the arena of the world
45 proletarian revolution'. According to this plan there is but one prospect left for our revolution: to vegetate in its own contradictions and rot away while waiting for the world revolution.

What is the dictatorship of the proletariat according to Lenin?

The dictatorship of the proletariat is a power which rests on an
50 alliance between the proletariat and the labouring masses of the peasantry for 'the complete overthrow of capital' and for 'the final establishment and consolidation of socialism'.

What is the dictatorship of the proletariat according to Trotsky?

The dictatorship of the proletariat is a power which comes 'into
55 hostile collision' with 'the broad masses of the peasantry' and seeks the solution of its 'contradictions' only 'in the arena of the world proletarian revolution'.

What difference is there between this theory of 'permanent revolution' and the well-known theory of Menshevism which
60 repudiates the concept of dictatorship of the proletariat? Essentially there is no difference. There can be no doubt at all. 'Permanent revolution' is not a mere underestimation of the revolutionary potentialities of the peasant movement. 'Permanent revolution' is an underestimation of the peasant movement which leads to the
65 repudiation of Lenin's theory of the dictatorship of the proletariat.
'The October revolution and the tactics of the Russian communists' reprinted in: J. V. Stalin *Works* vol. 6, p. 385.

(d) Trotsky's arguments

All are in agreement upon three fundamental propositions: the workers' state cannot stand unless it overthrows imperialism in the west; in Russia the conditions are not yet ripe for socialism; the
70 problems of socialist revolution are international in essence. If alongside these views which were to be condemned in seven or eight years as heresy, there had existed in the party other views, now recognised as orthodox and traditional, they would certainly have found expression in that Moscow conference and in the
75 congress of the party which preceded it. But neither the principal speaker nor those who took part in the debate – nor the newspaper

reports – suggest by a word the presence in the party of Bolshevik views opposing these 'Trotskyist' ones.

At the general city conference in Kiev, preceding the party
80 congress, the principal speaker Gorovitz said, 'The struggle for the salvation of our revolution can be waged only on an international scale. Two prospects lie before us: if the revolution conquers we will create the transitional state to socialism, if not we will fall under the power of international imperialism'. After the party congress,
85 at the beginning of August, Piatakov said at a new congress in Kiev, 'From the very beginning of the revolution, we have asserted that the destiny of the Russian proletariat is completely dependent upon the course of the proletarian revolution in the west . . . We are thus entering the stage of permanent revolution'. Commenting on
90 Piatakov's report, Gorovitz, already known to us, declared, 'I am in complete accord with Piatakov in his definition of our revolution as permanent'. But perhaps these two speakers represented a minority? No. Nobody opposed them upon this fundamental question.

Trotsky *op. cit*, pp. 388–9.

Questions

a What arguments does Stalin put forward against the idea of revolutionary war in extract (**a**)?

★ b What was 'Comrade Lenin's proposal' (line 17)?

c How were Trotsky's ideas proved wrong according to extract (**b**)?

d In extract (**c**), how is Trotsky supposed to have misinterpreted Lenin?

★ e Why does Stalin quote Lenin in extract (**c**)?

f How well does Trotsky defend his views in extract (**d**)?

★ g Outline the theory of permanent revolution. Why did it prove unpopular in Russia?

3 Left and Right Opposition

(a) Stalin on factionalism

'Whoever', says Lenin, 'weakens in the least the iron discipline of the Party of the proletariat actually aids the bourgeoisie against the proletariat.'

But from this it follows that the existence of factions is compati-
5 ble neither with the Party's unity nor with its iron discipline. It scarcely needs proof that the existence of factions leads to the existence of a number of centres and the existence of a number of centres means the absence of one common centre in the Party, the breaking up of unity of will, the weakening and disintegration of

10   discipline, the weakening and disintegration of the dictatorship. Of
course the parties of the Second International which are fighting
against the dictatorship of the proletariat and have no desire to lead
the proletarians to power can afford such liberalism as freedom of
factions for they have no need at all for iron discipline. But the
15   parties of the Communist International, whose activities are con-
ditioned by the task of achieving and consolidating the dictatorship
of the proletariat, cannot afford to be 'liberal' or to permit freedom
of factions.

The Party represents unity of will which precludes all factional-
20   ism and division of authority in the Party.

Hence Lenin's demand for the 'complete elimination of all
factionalism' and the 'immediate dissolution of all groups without
exception that have been formed on the basis of various platforms',
on pain of 'unconditional and immediate expulsion from the party'.

Stalin, J. V. (1970) *The Foundations of Leninism* (Peking:
Foreign Languages Press) pp. 114–15.

(b) Trotsky, Zinoviev and Kamanev

25   STOLBERG: Mr Trotsky, the first mistake that Zinoviev there
speaks of, you characterise as his opposition to the October
Revolution. Wasn't it rather an opposition to the October insurrection?

TROTSKY: To the October Revolution because without the
30   October insurrection, it could not become the October Revolution.

GOLDMAN: How long did your bloc with Zinoviev and Kamanev last?

TROTSKY: Almost two years – nineteen months to be exact. It
began in the Spring of 1926 and finished in the Fall of 1927.

35   GOLDMAN: What was the occasion of the split between the
forces of Zinoviev and Kamanev and your own?

TROTSKY: The reason was the repressions of the bureaucracy
against the Opposition. At the beginning it was possible, it seemed
possible, that Zinoviev and Kamanev, to Zinoviev and Kamanev –
40   we had great discussions about this – that by our fight we could
change in a short time the policy of the Party. The reaction in the
masses and the active reaction in the bureaucracy showed that it
was impossible. The bureaucracy became hardened and persecuted
the Opposition. Then the question was: Break with the bureaucracy
45   and the apparatus, with legal existence or go back and capitulate.

GOLDMAN: Did the break-up of your block with Zinoviev
occur after or before your expulsion from the party?

TROTSKY: Before, some weeks before, but not formally. It was
clear to us, and we were prepared for the expulsion. It was clear
50   that my group was totally ready to accept the expulsion; that the
Zinoviev group would avoid the expulsion at any price.

GOLDMAN: Did the Zinoviev group succeed in avoiding expulsion?

TROTSKY: Not immediately by the capitulation. They remained
55 six months expelled from the party.

GOLDMAN: At the congress where you were expelled, were
they also expelled?

TROTSKY: Yes, all the Oppositionists were expelled, in spite of
the capitulation.

60 FINERTY: Mr Goldman, Commissioner Stolberg thinks it would
be as well also to show what was the basis of the bloc between
Trotsky and Zinoviev.

TROTSKY: The basis is formulated in our platform published
also in English in a book under the title, 'The Real Situation in
65 Russia'. It is an important document of 150 pages embracing all the
questions of social and political life in the Soviet Union, of its
international policy and questions of the Communist International.
As I explained, it was a question of democracy against bureaucracy,
equality against privileges, more industrialisation – at that time the
70 bureaucracy was against industrialisation – for collectivisation in
villages, an international revolutionary policy as against a narrow
national policy in diplomacy, a total change in the policy of the
Communist International, more independence in the sections of the
Comintern, and at the same time more of an international revolu-
75 tionary policy of the sections.

Case of Leon Trotsky, *op. cit.*, pp. 82–3.

(c) Stalin on Trotsky's failings

What is the main sin of the opposition which determined the
bankruptcy of its policy? Its main sin is that it tried, is trying, and
will go on trying to embellish Leninism with Trotskyism and to
replace Leninism with Trotskyism. There was a time when Kama-
80 nev and Zinoviev defended Leninism from Trotsky's attacks. At
that time Trotsky himself was not so bold. That was one line.
Later, however, Zinoviev and Kamanev, frightened by new difficulties, deserted to Trotsky's side, formed something in the nature
of an inferior August bloc with him and thus became captives of
85 Trotskyism. That was further confirmation of Lenin's earlier
statement that the mistake Zinoviev and Kamanev made in
October was not 'accidental'. From fighting for Leninism, Zinoviev and Kamanev went over to the line of fighting for Trotskyism. That is an entirely different line. And that indeed explains why
90 Trotsky has now become bolder.

The opposition thinks that its defeat can be 'explained' by the
personal factor, by Stalin's rudeness, by the obstinacy of Bukharin
and Rykov and so forth. That is too cheap an explanation. It is an
incantation not an explanation – Trotsky has been fighting Lenin-

95   ism since 1904. From 1904 until the February revolution in 1917 he
hung around the Mensheviks desperately fighting Lenin's party all
the time. During that period Trotsky suffered a number of defeats
at the hands of Lenin's party. Why? Perhaps Stalin's rudeness was
to blame? But Stalin was not yet the Secretary of the Central
100 Committee at the time; he was not abroad but in Russia fighting
tsarism underground, whereas the struggle between Trotsky and
Lenin raged abroad. So what had Stalin's rudeness to do with it?
     During the period from the October revolution to 1922 Trotsky,
already a member of the Bolshevik party, managed to make two
105 grand sorties against Lenin and his party: in 1918 – on the question
of the Brest peace; and in 1921 – on the trade union question. Both
those sorties ended in Trotsky being defeated. Why? Perhaps
Stalin's rudeness was to blame here? But at that time Stalin was not
yet the Secretary of the Central Committee. The secretarial posts
110 were then occupied by the notorious Trotskyists. So what had
Stalin's rudeness got to do with it?
     Later Trotsky made a number of fresh sorties against the Party
(1923, 1924, 1926, 1927) and each sortie ended in Trotsky suffering
a fresh defeat.
115   Is it not obvious from all this that Trotsky's fight against the
Leninist Party has deep far-reaching historical roots? Is it not
obvious from this that the struggle the Party is now waging against
Trotskyism is a continuation of the struggle that the Party headed
by Lenin waged from 1904 onwards?
120   Is it not obvious from all this that the attempts of the Trotskyists
to replace Leninism by Trotskyism are the chief cause of the failure
and bankruptcy of the entire line of the opposition?
          'The Trotskyist opposition, before and now', October
          23, 1927, reprinted in: J. V. Stalin *Works* vol. 10,
          pp. 101–2

(d) Stalin on Bukharin

Bukharin's starting point is not a rapid rate of development of
industry as the lever for the reconstruction of agriculture but the
125 development of individual peasant farming. He puts in the foreground the 'normalisation' of the market and permission for the
free play of prices on the agricultural produce market, complete
freedom for private trade. Hence his distrustful attitude to the
collective farms which manifested itself in his speech at the July
130 plenum of the Central Committee and in his theses prior to that
July plenum. Hence his disapproval of any form of emergency
measures against the kulaks during grain procurement.
     We know that Bukharin shuns emergency measures as the devil
shuns holy water.
135   We know that Bukharin is still unable to understand that under

present conditions the kulak will not supply a sufficient quantity of grain voluntarily of his own accord.

That has been proved by our two years' experience of grain-procurement work.

140 But what if, in spite of everything, there is not enough marketable grain? To this Bukharin replies: Do not worry the kulaks with emergency measures; import grain from abroad. Not long ago he proposed that we import about 50 000 000 poods of grain, i.e. to the value of about 100 000 000 rubles in foreign currency. But what

145 if foreign currency is required to import equipment for industry? To this Bukharin replies: Preferences must be given to grain imports – thus evidently relegating imports of equipment for industry to the background.

It follows therefore that the basis for the solution of the grain

150 problem and for the reconstruction of agriculture is not a rapid rate of development of industry but the development of individual peasant farming including kulak farming on the basis of a free market and the free play of prices in the market.

'The Right Deviation in the CPSU', speech of April 1929, reprinted in: J. V. Stalin, *Works*, vol. 12, pp. 64–5.

Questions

a   What were the dangers of factionalism, according to extract (**a**)?
★ b   Why did Stalin put forward the views expressed in this extract?
★ c   Did Lenin and Stalin have the same views on what constituted factionalism?
d   In extract (**b**), what were the arguments of Trotsky and his allies against Stalin?
e   How far is extract (**b**) supportive of Zinoviev?
★ f   In extract (**c**) why did Kamanev and Zinoviev 'desert to Trotsky's side' (line 83)?
g   What arguments does extract (**c**) give to explain Trotsky's failure?
h   Why did Stalin oppose Bukharin according to extract (**d**)?
★ i   Outline the opposing views of Trotsky and Bukharin in the 1920s.

4   Stalin's success

(a) The Party triumphs

We must affirm that the party had fought a serious fight against the Trotskyites, rightists and bourgeois nationalists, and that it disarmed ideologically all the enemies of Leninism. This ideological fight was carried on successfully as a result of which the Party

5 became strengthened and tempered. Here Stalin played a positive role.

The Party led a great political ideological struggle against those in its own ranks who proposed anti-Leninist theses, who represented a political line hostile to the Party, and to the cause of
10 socialism. This was a stubborn and a difficult fight, but a necessary one, because the political lines of both the Trotskyite–Zinovievite bloc and of the Bukharinites led actually towards the restoration of capitalism and capitulation to the world bourgeoisie. Let us consider for a moment what would have happened if in 1928 to
15 1929 the political line of right deviation had prevailed among us or orientation towards 'cotton-dress industrialisation' or towards the kulak etc. We would not now have a powerful heavy industry, we would not have the kolkhozes, we would find ourselves disarmed and weak in a capitalist encirclement.
20 It was for this reason that the Party led an inexorable ideological fight and explained to all Party members, and to the non-Party masses, the harm and the danger of the anti-Leninist proposals of the Trotskyite opposition, and the right opportunists. And this great work of explaining the Party line bore fruit; both the
25 Trotskyites and the right opportunists were politically isolated; the overwhelming Party majority supported the Leninist line and the Party was able to awaken and organise the working masses to apply the Leninist Party line and to build socialism.
Worth noting is the fact that even during the progress of the
30 furious ideological fight against the Trotskyites, the Zinovievites, the Bukharinites, and others, extreme repressive measures were not used against them. The fight was on ideological grounds.

Khrushchev, *op. cit.*, p. 587

(b) How Stalin won

Lenin suffered the first attack from arteriosclerosis in May 1922. But the revolution had been afflicted with hardening of the arteries
35 for over three years. In 1917 power had been seized by Lenin under the slogan of the dictatorship of the proletariat. Step by step during the following four years it was transformed into a one-party dictatorship. In the ruling Bolshevik organisation these steps were marked by the following guideposts:

40   First – the Seventh congress of the party in 1918, which ratified the dishonourable peace with the Central Powers, also declared that the primary and fundamental task was the taking of the most energetic relentless decisive and Draconian measures for the raising of party discipline, the creation of iron cohorts of
45   proletarians and universal military training of the entire adult population, irrespective of sex.
       Second – that congress elected a commission of seven, which comprised Lenin, Trotsky and Stalin, to frame a new constitution

for the parts, which was then renamed from Bolshevik to
50 Communist. This ironclad constitution is still in force.
Third – the power conferred upon party members made hundreds of thousands of non-revolutionists join its ranks in order to
become officials and bred, during the period of military communism, bureaucratic wantonness and misrule.
55 Fourth – the suppression of all opposition within the party,
particularly the first workers' groups that fought for freedom of
opinion and democratic control of the political machines, established the precedent that all criticism was counter-revolutionary.
Unity became an aim and not a means.
60 Fifth – the Central Committee was enlarged to include two score
leaders. Its executive power was transferred to the small Political
Bureau. The once supreme highest organ became in reality a
Sanhedrin of a consultative nature.
Sixth – the instrument of terror, the Cheka, created to combat
65 counter-revolution against the state, was turned into a party
weapon for the cruel and unscrupulous destruction of all non-
Bolshevik groups and for the rooting out of heresy within the
Bolshevik household.

The effects upon the state structure of the policies pursued during
70 the civil war were just as profound in the life of the revolution.
They were as follows:

First – the Soviet government had a coalition with the Left–
Socialist–Revolutionaries during the first year of its existence.
This is not generally realised. It was not until 1919 that the non-
75 Bolshevik commissars were forced out from Lenin's cabinet.
The council of peoples' commissars then became a training
school for statesmanship under Lenin's guidance. Its power was
transferred to the Political Bureau.
Second – the Soviets of workers and peasants, which were in the
80 beginning representative bodies, although elected without secret
and universal suffrage, were gradually transferred into
bureaucratic civil-service departments adjuncts of the party dictatorship. But it was not until the climax of military communism
that the minority socialist deputies in the Soviets were silenced,
85 dispersed, exiled, imprisoned, and finally eliminated completely.
Third – the capitalist press was not destroyed until 1918. The
socialist newspapers and magazines languished until the spring of
1919. It was at the end of that year that freedom of assembly for
non-Bolshevik revolutionaries was abolished.
90 Fourth – the trade unions retained their independence with a
certain measure of internal freedom and democracy until the
height of military communism. It was then that Trotsky proposed the militarisation of labour. Lenin and Stalin opposed for

95 tactical reasons this 'state-isation' policy but the labour unions became in fact, if not in name, obedient state organs.

Fifth – the taxation of the peasant assumed the form of forcible requisition of his produce, frequently by means of armed detachments. The fight against the kulak with the aid of the poorer peasants grew out of economic necessity. It was justified by the 100 theory of promoting the hegemony of the proletariat, but it alienated the great majority of the agricultural toilers of the country.

Such were some of the developments of the period of military communism in the organism of the dictatorship. Without these, 105 Stalin would never have had his opportunity.

Levine, *op. cit.*, pp. 169–70.

(c) Another opinion

The whole strength of Stalin's position was that he was General Secretary of the Party (it has no President) and that the Party governed Russia. He, more than anyone else, was the real distributor of posts – even in the Soviet Cabinet to which he himself never 110 belonged. He kept the books, he knew all the records – all the qualities, weaknesses and aspirations of his fellow-members. Stalin's methods in council were very different from Trotsky's, though he made long, clear and detailed expositions of policy, both in speeches and in writings. They were those of a business man. He 115 did not harangue his colleagues when in council, he carefully followed all that was said, and, by the time that he summed up, he was able to take his stand on ground where he knew he would be supported (at least that is the record of Bazhanov one of the secretaries of the Politburo). Trotsky might make the moves and 120 the mistakes and Stalin would wait for him and outplay him. Lenin has left his opinion of both men: Trotsky a kind of mountebank, of whom you cold never be certain; Stalin, one who might spoil everything by his roughness.

Pares, Bernard (1940) *Russia* (Harmondsworth: Penguin books) p. 140.

Questions

a Why, according to extract (*a*), was it a good thing that Stalin triumphed in the struggle for power?

b 'The fight was on ideological grounds' (line 4). Was this true?

c What part did Lenin play in Stalin's rise to power, according to extract (*b*)?

★ d Using extracts (*b*) and (*c*) and any other information known to you, how was it that Stalin succeeded in the struggle for power?

III Socialism in One Country

Introduction

It was widely agreed in the mid-1920s that Lenin's early death had left many decisions unresolved. One of the most important concerned the economy. Russia still retained a primitive system of agriculture, which barely provided sufficient food at the best of times, and an industrial output that lagged well behind that of its smaller, but more advanced, Western competitors. Under Lenin, various piecemeal solutions had been tried, but without great success. In 1924, the year Lenin died, the country was working under the New Economic Policy which was based on the non-communist principle of private profit. The peasants were encouraged to grow more food, without having to change their farming practices, and without forcing them to become communist; the industrial entrepreneurs, or Nepmen, developed only light industries which needed the least investment of time and money before showing a profit. Modern productive methods in farming, true communist control of the peasantry, and advanced heavy industry were still nowhere in sight.

Stalin's avowed policy of Socialism in one country – the idea that Russia could and must survive on its own in a world full of enemies – laid even greater emphasis on the need for a modern and resilient economy. Most agreed on the necessity for this, but both then and now there was much debate on the value and morality of Stalin's methods and the eventual worth of this drive for modernisation. By the late 1930s, farming had been collectivised, and to a certain extent modernised, but the determined opposition of the peasants (notably in the mass extermination of their livestock) meant that food production actually declined dramatically in the years immediately following the move to collectives. In industry, the arbitrary, and often wildly optimistic, quotas imposed from above produced not only much hardship to the workers but also a great deal of equipment that did not work: all too often quality was sacrificed to quantity. Consumer goods received a very low, or even non-existent, priority.

Even Stalin accepted that some mistakes were made in this rush to modernise (although naturally he attached little blame to himself). Yet by the late 1930s, after much agony and suffering, the economy was becoming more modern. Unfortunately it was at this point that World War II hit Russia.

1 Agriculture

(a) Stalin on farming success

Here are some figures.

In 1928 the crop area of the state farms amounted to 1 425 000 hectares with a marketable grain output of more than 6 000 000 centners (over 36 000 000 poods), and the crop area of the
5   collective farms amounted to 1 390 000 hectares with a marketable grain output of about 3 500 000 centners.

In the coming year, 1930, the crop area of the state farms according to the plan will probably amount to 3 280 000 hectares with a marketable grain output of 18 000 000 centners and the crop
10   area of the collective farms will certainly amount to 15 000 000 hectares with a marketable grain output of about 49 000 000 centners.

This unprecedented success in the development of collective farming is due to a variety of causes of which the following at least
15   should be mentioned.

It is due first of all to the fact that the Party carried out Lenin's policy of educating the masses by consistently leading the masses of the peasantry to collective farming through implanting a co-operative communal life. It is due to the fact that the Party waged
20   a successful struggle against those who tried to run ahead of the movement and force the development of collective farming by decrees (the Left phrasemongers) as well as those who tried to drag the Party back and remain in the wake of the movement (the Right blockheads). Had it not pursued such a policy, the Party
25   would not have been able to transform the collective farm movement into a real mass movement of the peasants themselves.

Secondly, this unprecedented success in agricultural development is due to the fact that the Soviet government correctly recognised the growing needs of the peasants for modern imple-
30   ments, for modern technique; it correctly recognised that the old forms of cultivation leave the peasantry in a hopeless position, and taking all this into account it came to their aid in good time by organising machine-hiring stations, tractor columns, and machine and tractor stations; by organising collective cultivation of the
35   land, by establishing collective farms and finally by having the state farms give every assistance to peasant farming.

Lastly, this unprecedented success in collective-farm development is due to the fact that the matter was taken in hand by the

advanced workers of the country. I am referring to the workers
40 brigades, tens and hundreds of which are scattered in the principal
regions of the country. It must be acknowledged that of all existing
and potential propagandists of the collective-farm movement
among the peasant masses, the worker propagandists are the best.

What can be surprising in the fact that the workers have
45 succeeded in convincing the peasants of the advantages of largescale collective farming over individual small farming, the more so
as the collective farms and state farms are striking examples of
these advantages?

'A year of great change', 2 November 1929, reprinted in
J. V. Stalin, *Works*, vol. 12, p. 120

(b) Over enthusiasm?

The main link of the collective-farm movement, its predominant
50 form at the present moment, the link which has to be grasped now,
is the agricultural artel.

In the agricultural artel the basic means of production primarily
for grain production – labour use of the land machines and other
implements, draught animals and farm buildings – are socialised.
55 In the artel the household plots (small vegetable gardens, small
orchards), the dwelling houses, a part of the dairy cattle, small
livestock, poultry etc. are not socialised.

The artel is the main link of the collective-farm movement
because it is the form best adapted for solving the grain problem.
60 And the grain problem is the main link in the whole system of
agriculture because if it is not solved it will be impossible to solve
either the problem of stock-breeding (small and large) or the
problem of the industrial and social crops that provide the
principal raw materials for industry. That is why the agricultural
65 artel is the main link in the system of the collective-farm movement at the present moment.

Can it be said that this line of the Party is being carried out
without violation or distortion? No, it cannot, unfortunately. We
know that in a number of areas in the USSR, where the struggle
70 for the existence of the collective farms is still far from over and
where artels are not yet consolidated, attempts are being made to
skip the artel framework and to leap straight away into the
agricultural commune. The artel is still not consolidated but they
are already 'socialising' dwelling houses, small livestock and
75 poultry; moreover this 'socialisation' is degenerating into bureaucratic decreeing on paper because the conditions which would
make such socialisation necessary do not yet exist. One might
think that the grain problem has already been solved in the
collective farms, that it is already a past stage, that the principal
80 task at the present moment is not solution of the grain problem but

solution of the problem of livestock and poultry breeding. Who, we may ask, benefits from this blockheaded 'work' of lumping together different forms of the collective farm movement? Who benefits from this running too far ahead which is stupid and
85 harmful to our cause? Irritating the collective-farm peasant by 'socialising' dwelling houses, all dairy cattle, all small livestock and poultry, when the grain problem is still unsolved, when the artel form of collective-farming is not yet consolidated – is it not obvious that such a policy can be to the satisfaction and advantage
90 only of our sworn enemies?

How could there have arisen in our midst such block-headed exercises in 'socialisation', such ludicrous attempts to overleap oneself, attempts which aim at by-passing classes and the class struggle and which in fact bring grist to the mill of our class
95 enemies?

They could have arisen only as a result of the blockheaded belief of a section of our Party: 'We can achieve anything!', 'There's nothing we can't do!'

They could have arisen only because some of our Comrades
100 have become dizzy with success and for the moment have lost clearness of mind and sobriety of vision.

To correct the line of our work in the sphere of collective-farm development we must put an end to these sentiments.

That is now one of the immediate tasks of the Party.
105 The art of leadership is a serious matter. One must not lag behind the movement because to do so is to lose contact with the masses. But neither must one run too far ahead, because to run too far ahead is to lose the masses and isolate oneself. He who wants to lead a movement and at the same time keep in touch with
110 the vast masses must wage a fight on two fronts – against those who lag behind and those who run too far ahead.

'Dizzy with success', 2 March 1930, reprinted in: J. V. Stalin, *Works*, vol. 12, pp. 203–4.

Questions

a What successes in agriculture are revealed by the statistics in extract (**a**)?

★ b Who does Stalin mean when he refers to 'Left phrasemongers' (line 22) and 'Right blockheads' (line 24)?

c According to extract (**a**), what part did the following play in the success: the government; workers; peasants?

d In extract (**b**), what are the differences between the agricultural artel and the commune?

e According to this extract, what are the problems facing agriculture at this time and how have they been caused?

★ f What does extract (**b**) reveal about Stalin's attitude towards the failure of his plans?

(c) An optimistic view of collectivisation

Without expecting to convince the prejudiced, we give, for what it may be deemed worth, the conclusion to which our visits in 1932 and 1934 and subsequent examination of the available evidence now lead us. That in each of the years 1931 and 1932 there was a
5 partial failure of crops in various parts of the huge area of the USSR is undoubtedly true. It is true, also, of British India and of the United States. It has been true, also, of the USSR and of every other country of comparable size, in each successive year of the present century. In countries of such vast extent, having every
10 kind of climate, there is always a partial failure of crops some-where. How extensive and how serious was this partial failure of crops in the USSR, in 1931 and 1932, it is impossible to ascertain with any assurance. On the one hand it has been asserted by people who have seldom had any opportunity of going to the
15 suffering districts, that throughout huge provinces there ensued a total absence of foodstuffs, so that (as in 1891 and 1892) literally several millions of people died of starvation. On the other hand, Soviet officials on the spot, in one district after another, informed the present writers that, whilst there was a shortage and hunger,
20 there was at no time a total lack of bread, though its quality was impaired by using other ingredients than wheaten flour; and that any increase in the death-rate due to disease accompanying defective nutrition occurred in only a relatively small number of villages. What may carry more weight than this official testimony
25 was that of various resident British and American journalists who travelled during 1933 and 1934 through the districts reputed to be the worst affected and who declared to the present writers that they had found no reason to suppose that the trouble had been more serious than was officially represented. Our own impression,
30 after considering all the available evidence, is that the partial failure of crops certainly extended to only a fraction of the USSR; possibly to no more than one-tenth of the geographical area. We think it plain that this partial failure was not in itself sufficiently serious to cause actual starvation, except possibly in the worst
35 districts, relatively small in extent.

This is not to deny that there were whole districts in which drought or cold seriously reduced the yield. But there are clearly other cases, how many we cannot pretend to estimate, in which the harvest failures were caused not by something in the sky but by
40 something in the collective farm itself. And we are soon put on the track of discovery. As we have already mentioned, we find a leading personage in the direction of the Ukrainian revolt actually claiming that, 'the opposition of the Ukrainian people', caused the failure of the grain-storing plan of 1931 and still more so that of
45 1932. He boasts of the success of the 'passive resistance which aimed at a systematic frustration of the Bolshevik plan for the

sewing and gathering of the harvest'. He tells us plainly that owing
to the efforts of himself and his friends, whole tracts were left
unsewn, and, in addition, when the crop was being gathered last
50 year (1932), it happened that in many areas especially in the south,
20, 40, and even 50 per cent was left in the fields and was either not
collected at all or was ruined in the threshing.

So far as the Ukraine was concerned, it is clearly not Heaven
which is principally to blame for the failure of the crops but the
55 misguided members of many of the collective farms.

Webb, Sidney and Beatrice (1935) *Soviet Communism, A
New Civilisation*, (London: Longman, Green and Co.)
pp. 200–1.

(d) An opposing viewpoint

What were the mistakes which, in Postyschev's view, led to the
fiasco of the previous year's grain collection? This was not due to
the 'objective causes' (dimunition of the harvest famine etc) but to
the 'leniency' with which the local authorities discharged their duty
60 · of taking the grain from the producers. To illustrate this harmful
'leniency' he quoted a number of examples, e.g. a regulation
issued by the Odessa district committee that the first hectare
harvested 'was to be kept available for local or public consumption'. Postyschev commented on this as follows: 'Need I waste
65 words in pointing out how wrong such an instruction is which
assigns a secondary position to the delivery of grain to the state
while the feeding of the community is placed first? Is it not the best
possible proof that some of our district committees were in-
fluenced by consumers' interests, thus promoting the class in-
70 terests of our enemies to the detriment of the proletarian state?
Can such leniency strengthen our system of collectivisation? No;
the Bolshevik struggle has no room for such leniency'.

Surely these words reveal the whole tragedy of the situation
more clearly than any reports.

Armende, Dr E. (1936) *Human life in Russia*, (London:
George Allen and Unwin Ltd) p. 60

(e) An American opinion, 1938

75 Even more significant than the mineral wealth of such a territory
are its agricultural resources. Such wealth is inexhaustible. It
renews itself each year.

In 1937 the total area under cultivation in the Soviet Union was
367 170 949 acres. This is in contrast to 327 661 000 (1935) acres in
80 the United States and 56 134 000 acres in Canada. Of the entire
population, about 65 per cent are engaged in agriculture. It is
interesting to note that in 1913 57 per cent of the total output of

Russian industry was agricultural, whereas industrial output constituted but 43 per cent. In 1937, however, the industrial output
85 comprised 77 per cent of the total output in contrast to the remainder 23 per cent of agriculture, which quantitively was slightly in excess of 1913. Generally speaking, the agricultural output in the Soviet Union under the present regime has not been in excess of pre-revolutionary production. In 1937, however, there
90 was a bumper crop which broke all records. The cereal crop for that year is estimated to be about 111 384 000 metric tons. It should be borne in mind in this connection that a great effort was made by the planning authorities to diversify agriculture, which eliminated large areas of cereal coverage and diverted them to the
95 development of new crops such as cotton, sugar beet, etc.

The following data indicate the remarkable agricultural wealth of this country.

Wheat. In 1935 the Soviet Union produced one-third of the total wheat crop of the world. It was two and a half times greater than
100 that produced in the United States; four times as much as Canada.

Cattle. The average number of cattle in the Soviet Union between 1926–30 was 64 900 000 in contrast to the 59 191 000 in the United States. It was larger than the combined herds of
105 Argentina and Germany. During the 'strike' of the agricultural classes during the collectivisation period from 1929–33, the number of cattle had declined to 38 400 000 in 1933. By 1935 it had increased to 49 255 000.

Livestock: sheep, swine, horses. During the same period there was
110 an enormous decline in these herds. They were practically cut in two. By 1935 there had been an increase of about 20 per cent over the low period but still in 1935 the percentage of these herds was from 30 to 40 per cent less than in 1928.

Davies, Joseph E. (1942) *Mission to Moscow* (London: Victor Gollancz) pp. 245–6.

Questions

a In what ways does extract (*c*) attempt to minimise the crop failure in Russia?
b Who was to blame for the crop failure, according to extract (*d*)?
c Does extract (*e*) judge Russian farming methods to have been a success?
★ d Why do you think extracts (*c*), (*d*) and (*e*) all take different views on Russian agriculture?

2 Industry

(a) Stalin's assessment

And we have not only created these new great industries but have
created them on a scale and in dimensions that eclipse the scale and
dimensions of European industry.

And, as a result of all this, the capitalist elements have been
5 completely and irrevocably ousted from industry, and socialist
industry has become the sole form of industry in the USSR.

And, as a result of all this, our country has become converted
from an agrarian into an industrial country; for the proportion of
industrial output as compared with agricultural output has risen
10 from 48 per cent of the total, in the beginning of the five year plan
period (1928), to 70 per cent at the end of the fourth year of the five
year plan period (1932).

And, as a result of all this, we have succeeded by the end of the
fourth year of the five year plan period in fulfilling the total
15 programme of industrial output, which was drawn up for five
years to the extent of 93.7 per cent, thereby raising the volume of
industrial output to more than three times the pre-war output, and
to more than double the level of 1928. As for the programme of
output for heavy industry, we have fulfilled the five year plan by
20 108 per cent.

It is true that we are six per cent short of fulfilling the total
programme of the five year plan. But that is due to the fact that in
the view of the refusal of neighbouring countries to sign pacts of
non-aggression with us, and of the obligations that arose in the Far
25 East, we were obliged for the purpose of strengthening our
defence, hastily to switch a number of factories to the production of
modern defensive means. And, owing to the necessity of going
through a certain period of preparation, this switch resulted in these
factories suspending production for four months, which could not
30 but affect the fulfillment of the total programme of output for 1932,
as fixed in the five year plan. As a result of this operation, we have
completely filled the gaps with regard to the defensive capabilities
of this country. But this was bound to affect adversely the
fulfillment of the programme of output provided in the five year
35 plan. It is beyond any doubt that, but for this incidental circumstance, we would almost certainly not only have fulfilled, but
even over-fulfilled the total production figures of the five year
plan.

Finally, as a result of all this, the Soviet Union has been
40 converted from a weak country, unprepared for defence into a
country mighty in defence, a country prepared for every conting-
ency, a country capable of producing on a mass scale all modern
means of defence, and of equipping its army with them in the event
of an attack from abroad.

45   Such, in general terms, are the results of the five year plan, in
four years in the sphere of industry.

> 'The results of the first five year plan', 7 January 1933,
> reprinted in J. V. Stalin, *Works*, pp. 183–4.

(b) Methods of industrialisation

The plan had been designed in consultation with the best engineers
from the United States, Britain, France and Germany. Under the
five year plan, the Soviet Government had been almost profligate in
50   paying any amount of money to get the best engineering, technical
and planning skill that any of the western countries could offer.
This plant had been built in 1931. Approximately 60 per cent of its
machinery had been built in the United States. We were advised
that there were then working at the plant some 9000 men and
55   women, including 121 technicians of various nationalities.
This period of the first five year plan was characterised by
alternative ruthless purges and oppressions, and conciliatory policies, for all of which Stalin was extolled. It is interesting to note
that the regime became confronted more and more by the necessity
60   of making a success of these enormous undertakings. Their con-
tinuance in power depended ultimately on making good the
promises made to the proletariat. In order to make good, and make
the system of industry work, there developed a marked and
continuing departure in practice from the communist principle.
65   The only insistent and constant stimulus to the workers was found
to be the profit motive. Concessions were also made in the
extension of rights of property to the peasants as well as to other
classes. The Stakhanovite movement became a national policy. By
1934 there appeared clearly a very notable advance in heavy
70   industry – both in much larger output and lesser costs.
Measurably, the five year plan had justified itself. The outstand-
ing fact in the situation, however, is that it was not because of
government operation of industry, but in spite of it. The enormous
wealth of the country practically ensured, quantitively, a large
75   measure of success despite the enormous inefficiencies, wastes and
losses which such a system must necessarily entail. What the
regime did do, however, was to conceive the plan and drive it
through. It is also significant, that in order to succeed, the regime
dropped the principle of communism in practical application.

> Davies, *op. cit.*, pp. 251–2.

(c) The example of Magnitogorsk

80   In the 'Times' atlas, in obscure print, you may find the place-name
Magnitnaya (Magnet Mountain), lying 617 metres above sea level,
and in the extreme south of the Ural Mountains. On the right bank

of the small river which skirted the mountain lay the Cossack village of Magnitnaya.

85 In 1929, windswept flowery meadows lay beyond the village. Herds of cattle browsed up the slope of the Attach Mountain. Today one of the world's supreme steel centres hums and roars where the cattle grazed. The Attach mountain was one vast lump of iron ore containing 63 per cent iron and weight 300 million

90 tons. The Magnet Mountain gives its appropriate name of Magnitogorsk.

An area of 54 square kilometres was selected for the site of Magnitogorsk. Five square kilometres were for the metallurgical plant.

Workers of thirty-five nationalities assembled and built barracks

95 for workers, a settlement for foreign specialists, co-operative stores, restaurants, hospitals, nurseries, clubs and a theatre. A ferro–concrete dam was thrown across the little river and a lake of 13½ square kilometres was formed. The work was done in winter, with slightly heated concrete, the first experiment of its kind in the world.

100 Aerodromes were built, railways cut, roads laid: tractors, trucks, automobiles, jostled with caravans of horses and camels on the new highways. Centuries were telescoped into months.

Sixty thousand workers settled, built two electric stations, a brickyard, a saw-mill, a wood-factory, a forge and a machine shop.

105 The attack upon the mountain began. Ledges 30 feet high were cut in it to get the ore.

Enormous structures arose; the housing of huge ore crushers; vast walls of the power plant; batteries of coke ovens and blast furnaces towering to the height of 150 feet.

110 The blast furnaces of Magnitogorsk form the most powerful battery in the world. The open hearth furnaces are the largest in the world.

Chemical works spring up to utilise the chemical by-products of the coke ovens; benzol, ammonia, coal-tar and fertilisers.

115 The city itself is planned with care: Soviet factories turn out men as well as steel: seventeen great blocks of buildings, each with its own department store, school, restaurant, and creches; each apartment in the blocks of flats with its own bath, running water, electric light, gas and central heating.

120 By 1934 the mills turned out about 10 million tons of cast iron. By 1937 this had grown to 14½ million tons. Steel increased from 9½ to upwards of 17½ million tons and rolled metal from 9 to 13 million tons.

> Johnson, Hewlett (1939) *The socialist sixth of the world*, (London: Victor Gollancz) pp. 188–9.

(d) Quality or quantity?

The quality of Soviet cars appears to be still giving great anxiety

125 and the Moscow correspondent of the *Daily Herald* on the 21st
August reported a Departmental Chief of the Gorki motor plant
quoted in the Soviet press as stating that, 'if we maintain standards
the works would close tomorrow'. It was further stated that
although hundreds of cars with defective parts were passed, the
130 waste, through admittedly spoiled parts, was 9000 tons of metal in
the first half of 1937. The officials of the Stalin Motor Factory in
Moscow and those of the works at Gorki have been severely
criticised and have been threatened with criminal proceedings for
their failure to maintain output. It was reported in September that
135 during the last eight months output had lagged behind the Plan to
the extent of 13 000 lorries and 5 500 cars. The present rate of output
of motor vehicles is approximately 200 000 per annum. The output
in Great Britain in 1936 was 461 352 whilst the United States
reached the colossal figure of 4 454 535. Russian production of
140 motor vehicles is therefore somewhat less than half of that of Great
Britain and about one-twentieth of the output of the United States.

> Citrine, Sir William (1938) *I search for truth in Russia* (Lon-
> don: George Routledge and Sons) p. 377.

Questions

a Why was it important that the five year plan should be a success,
   according to extract (*a*)?

b What reasons are given for this plan's partial failure?

★ *c* How valid are these reasons?

d According to extract (*b*), why did the first five year plan
   succeed?

e Is the author of extract (*b*) sympathetic towards Stalin's regime?

f What was the Stakhanovite movement (line 68)?

g Compare extracts (*c*) and (*d*) in their assessments of the success
   of the five year plans.

★ *h* Using these sources (*a*) to (*d*), and any other information
   known to you, explain how Russia avoided the worldwide
   depression of the 1930s.

3 Consequences

(a) Standards of living (i)

One further point remains to be recorded. The Russian peasant and
workman, who had formerly been tied to his patch of land or
factory bench until the end of his days, was granted two weeks'
holiday a year, with full pay. This concession was only recently
5 granted in Britain after widespread agitation extending over a
number of years. In Russia, of 1934, it must have represented an
unthought-of luxury.

During the summer months, special trains carried workmen and
their families to the Caucasian Riviera and the beauty spots of the
10 Crimea. The former haunts of an idle aristocracy, even their
ancient palaces and villas, were reconstructed to provide accommo-
dation for as many as possible of the new visitors.

By enactments like these, Stalin shows more clearly than by
words, how closely he is bound up with the Russian working
15 classes, from which he sprang, how well he knows their desires,
their prejudices, and their strength. Good treatment of workpeople
can increase factory production to an amazing degree, a fact which
Stalin always appreciated.

Cole *op. cit.*, p. 90

(b) Standards of living (ii)

As to the standard of life in Russia, whilst I have repeatedly said it is
20 rising, it is useless for anyone to deny the obvious fact that it is still
low, and in some respects deplorably so. So much of the national
income is devoted to capital equipment that there is not enough for
immediate consumption. The Russian workers evidently feel this
represents a sacrifice which is worthwhile. They are buoyed up
25 with confident hope for the future and the knowledge that their
standards are progressively improving. The psychological value of
this is immense and I believe it represents one of the greatest assets
that the Soviet government possesses.

The people see their country being equipped with plant and
30 machinery, which should one day rank it amongst the most
efficient in the world. They are desperately anxious to make
themselves independent, economically, of the capitalist states and
to furnish the means of effective defence should they be attacked.

Citrine *op. cit.*, p. 387.

(c) Standards of living (iii)

The 25 roubles a worker earned in 1913 did not buy much less than
35 the 370 roubles the Soviet worker made in 1939. This would mean
a very insignificant improvement of present earnings expressed in
money terms as compared with pre-war times. But it must be
considered that the pay of the different categories of workers varies
between 200 roubles, which is a minimum of existence, and 4000
40 roubles for the best qualified and most efficient categories of
specialists. In addition, the composition of the Soviet family is such
that a greater number of family members is gainfully employed
than was the case in pre-revolutionary times. The pooling of the
incomes of all family members often results in more satisfactory
45 averages.

As compared with other countries, the standard of living in the

Soviet Union is still very low. Workers abroad are better clad and housed than Soviet workers. On the other hand, the steady improvement of conditions in the USSR is incontestable. Unem-
50 ployment has been non-existent ever since the third year of the first five year plan. The watertight separation of the Soviet population from foreign sources of information, through censorship and prohibition of travelling for almost every Soviet citizen, the remembrance of former years of starvation, and intolerable hard-
55 ships which now have been overcome, account for a feeling of contentment with conditions of today, which is enhanced by the promise of an even brighter future.

USSR Handbook (1936) (London: Victor Gollancz), pp. 370–1.

Questions

a   According to extract (*a*), how and why did Stalin help the working classes?
b   Why did the Russian people accept a low standard of living, according to extract (*b*)?
c   Compare the assessments made of the Russian standard of living in extracts (*a*), (*b*) and (*c*).
★ d   Were the farming and industrial reforms of the 1930s, 'harsh but necessary'?

IV Government and Repression

Introduction

Mystery still surrounds many aspects of the purges of the mid 1930s. The official Party view of the time excused them by reference to the sudden murder of the rising star Sergei Kirov in 1934, an event that seemed to prove the existence of a hitherto unrecognised resistance to Stalin and the Communist government.

Purges had taken place at earlier dates. In the struggle for power, Trotsky, Zinoviev, and Kamanev, and a host of lesser officials, had been expelled from the Party. In the late 1920s, foreign experts drafted in to help with the five year plans had been put on trial for supposedly attempting to wreck the projects they were working upon. But these purges were minor affairs: foreign experts were merely expelled from the country, minor officials imprisoned; and by the early 1930s, Zinoviev and Kamanev, at least, were back in the Party.

The ferocity of the subsequent purges were quite unparalleled, at least within the Communist Party. These swiftly adopted a grim routine: arrests were made, leading figures put on trial – the Show Trials – where they confessed to anything in low monotonous voices and implicated other colleagues, who were, in turn, arrested. Most of Stalin's contemporaries were tried, found guilty, executed: Zinoviev, Kamanev, Bukharin, Rykov, Tomsky (although the latter committed suicide before sentencing). The purges extended sideways to include all the major figures in the armed forces and downwards to local party officials, in their hundreds of thousands. Finally the purges consumed many of those who had first organised them, including chief of police Yagoda.

Those outside of Russia were left with little positive proof of those condemned, other than the official and voluminous transcripts. Whether there was a genuine plot, mere paranoia on the part of Stalin, or ideas fabricated by outsiders (notably the theory that the German Gestapo wanted to weaken the Russian army) was hard to say. During this period Russia became almost impenetrable to outsiders, as the communists strengthened their control, and the Cult of Personality elevated Stalin to being not only all-powerful, but even all-knowing and all-wise.

1 The purges

(a) The official view of Trotsky's guilt

On December 1 1934 S. Kirov, a member of the Central Committee of the Communist Party of the Soviet Union and of the Praesidium of the Central Executive Committee, was killed in Leningrad. The subsequent investigation has established that the
5 murder was carried out by a member of an organisation formed to commit acts of terrorism against members of the Soviet Government and other leading figures. This was admitted in court at the end of December by Kirov's murderer and also by his accomplices. Supplementary investigations and the examinations in court con-
10 ducted in Moscow from 19 to 23 August 1936 further established that the said terrorist organisation was created on the initiative of Trotsky, now resident in Norway, who gave detailed instructions to his accomplices in the USSR for the murder of Stalin, Voroshilov, Kaganovich, Orjonikidze and other members of the Govern-
15 ment and leading figures. For this purpose, Trotsky sent special agents from abroad into the USSR. All these facts were confirmed in open court during the 1936 trial by all the accomplices and agents of Trotsky brought before the court. It may be thus regarded as established, that Trotsky, residing in Norway, is the organiser and
20 director of terrorist activities aimed at the murder of members of the Soviet Government and leaders of the Soviet people.

> 'Soviet demands for the expulsion of Trotsky from Norway, August 1936', reprinted in J. Degras, (ed.), *Soviet documents on foreign policy* vol. III, 1933–41, (Oxford University Press 1953) p. 204.

(b) Trotsky's defence

TROTSKY: I say we did not have a systematic – after 1931, a systematic communication with our friends in Russia. But from time to time we had correspondence in the persons of liberal
25 bureaucrats coming from Russia to Berlin and Paris who had conversations with our friends; and some even sent letters. They communicated on very interesting things. Then we used every foreigner sympathising with us, who went as tourist or guest to the Soviet anniversaries. We followed them up, and asked them that
30 they report to us when they got back.
FINERTY: Did you also give them written communications for that purpose?
TROTSKY: No; it was too dangerous for them and for our friends. I never proposed it, because it was unnecessary. What
35 could I say to them? I could not say anything to them that I could not say in my writings. You know I cannot invite an intermediary or a foreigner and say, 'Please kill Stalin; please kill Voroshilov'. It

is not my system of action. I can only say: 'Please communicate to me what is the mood of the workers, if you meet them in the factory. Or if you are in there, tell me if the American technique is really used by the Russians'. Because that is a greater historical perspective than the present duel with Stalin. But that is not the way the narrow bureaucracy looks at it.

FINERTY: Did you at any time subsequent to 1931 succeed in sending written communications into Russia?

TROTSKY: Yes. I explained we sent systematically postal cards with my personal point of view, my appreciations. Postal cards are not so severely controlled as letters. And we succeeded from time to time in 1930–31 or 1929–30. Very often we reached our friends by these cards. We received answers because it was the time when thousands and thousands of Oppositionists were simultaneously thrown into prisons and deportations. The GPU was not or did not control so strictly.

FINERTY: I am speaking after that period.

TROTSKY: After that period it became more and more difficult to have communications. They began to accuse everybody who was in communication with me by writing. I can present hundreds of postal cards from Russia. Then they began to accuse them of espionage.

Case of Leon Trotsky, *op. cit.*, pp. 262–3.

Questions

a According to extract (**a**) why should Trotsky be expelled from Russia?

b On what evidence did the Soviets base their accusations in this extract?

c Compare extracts (**a**) and (**b**) in their assessments of Trotsky's links with Russia.

★ d Why did Stalin make so many accusations against Trotsky?

(c) Show trials: Bukharin's final statement

Second question: Do you admit that the centre of the anti-Soviet organisation, of which you are a member, engaged in counter-revolutionary activities and set itself the aim of violently over-throwing the leadership of the Party and the government? I answered: Yes I admit it.

Third question: Do you admit that this centre engaged in terrorist activities, organised kulak uprisings and prepared for White guard kulak uprisings against members of the Political Bureau against the leadership of the Party and the Soviet power? I answered: It is true.

Fourth question: Do you admit that you are guilty of treasonable activities, as expressed in preparations for a conspiracy aiming at a *coup d'état*? I answered: Yes that is also true.

In court I admitted, and still admit, my guilt in respect to the crimes which I committed and of which I was accused by Citizen the State Prosecutor, at the end of the Court investigation and on the basis of the materials of the investigation in the possession of the Procurator. I declared also in court, and I stress and repeat it now, that I regard myself politically responsible for the sum total of the crimes committed by the bloc of Rights and Trotskyites.

I have merited the most severe punishment and I agree with Citizen the Procurator who several times repeated that I stand on the threshold of my hour of death.

Nevertheless I consider that I have the right to refute certain charges which were brought: a) in the printed Indictment; b) during the Court investigation; and c) in the speech for the prosecution made by Citizen the Procurator of the USSR.

I consider myself responsible for a grave and monstruous crime against the socialist fatherland and the whole international proletariat. I further consider myself responsible, both politically and legally, for wrecking activities, although, I personally do not remember having given directions about wrecking activities. I did not talk about this. I once spoke positively on this subject to Grinko. Even in my testimony, I mentioned that I had once told Radek that I considered this method of struggle as not very expedient. Yet Citizen the State Prosecutor makes me out to be a leader of the wrecking activities.

Citizen the Procurator explained in the speech for the prosecution that the members of a gang of brigands might commit robberies in different places, but that they would nevertheless be responsible for each other. That is true, but in order to be a gang the members of the gang of brigands must know each other and be in more or less close contact with each other. Yet I first learnt the name of Sharangovitch from the Indictment and I first saw him here in court. It was here that I first learnt of the existence of Maximov. I have never been acquainted with Pletnev. I have never been aquainted with Kazakov. I have never spoken about counter-revolutionary matters with Rakovsky. I have never spoken on this subject with Rosengoltz, and so on. Incidentally, even the Procurator did not ask me a single question about these people. Consequently the accused in this dock are not a group. They are confederates in a conspiracy along various lines, but they are not a group in the strict and legal sense of the word.

People's Commissariat of Justice in the USSR (1938) *Report of court proceedings in the case of the Anti-Soviet Bloc of Rights and Trotskyites* 2–13 March 1938 (Moscow) pp. 768–9.

(d) One view of army guilt

55 It was clear to me that Stalin had now determined to settle accounts with the Red Army opposition in the same bloody way that he had settled them with other opponents. The moment was opportune. The crisis of collectivisation had passed from an acute to a numbed chronic stage.

60 The Red Army generals had escaped the ordeal through which the political opposition had been passing for more than a dozen years. They lived outside that special party world in which people were for ever 'deviating' from the correct Stalinist course, 'recanting', 'deviating' again and again, 'recanting', each time with increasing penalties, and with a progressive breakdown of the will.

65 The job of the generals, the building of a powerful army and system of national defence had preserved their morale.

Stalin knew that Tukhachevsky, Gamarnik, Yakir, Uborevich and the other ranking generals could never be broken into the state of unquestioning obedience which he now required of all those

70 about him. They were men of great personal courage and he remembered during the days when his own prestige was at its lowest point, these generals, especially Tukhachevsky, had enjoyed enormous popularity, not only with the officers' corps and the rank and file of the army but with the people. He remembered too that

75 every critical stage of his rule – forcible collectivisation, hunger, rebellion, – the generals had supported him reluctantly, had put difficulties in his path, had forced deals upon him. He felt no certainty now that – confronted with his abrupt change of international policy – they would continue to recognise his totalitarian

80 authority.

> Krivitsky, W. G. (1939) *I was Stalin's agent* (London: Hamish Hamilton) p. 246.

(e) Another view

Facts are not now available, and it is doubtful whether they will be for a long time to come, which would justify a statement as to exactly what happened and just what constituted the 'offence' of these officers of the Red Army. Opinion must be based largely on

85 deductions from known facts and these are few. The press reports here are practically bare of anything except allegations. The same applies to Voroshilov's manifesto to the army. About all that has been stated is the position of the government, i.e. that these men were guilty of treason in the Red Army, had conspired with

90 Germany to overthrow the government, had admitted their guilt, had been tried by the cream of the Red Army – their own peers – and that the evidence of their guilt was submitted prior to the trials, to representative officers of all military districts of the Soviet

Union. That such a conference was in fact held, and that a very
large number of officers were present here in Moscow at the time,
seem to be confirmed by foreign military observers who saw many
of these Red Army officers, whom they had met in different parts
of the Soviet Union.

Davies, *op. cit.*, p. 136.

Questions

a   How argumentative is Bukharin in extract (*c*)?
★ b   What do you think was the purpose of his final statement?
c   Compare extracts (*d*) and (*e*) on the reasons for the trials of the
Red Army generals.
★ d   How trustworthy is the evidence given to support the arguments put forward in extract (*e*)?

(f) Interrogation tactics

The prison, at that time, says Ciliga, was full of engineer
'saboteurs'. Among them were several who had 'confessed'.

'Little by little, with great difficulty, I was able to learn the
history of their affairs, the history of the connection with 'sabotage'. 'They kept me five months in isolation', said one of them
who had confessed without papers, without anything to read,
without mail, without contact with the outside world; 'without
visits from my family; I was hungry I suffered from solitude; they
demanded of me that I confess having committed an act of sabotage
that never took place; I refused to take upon myself crimes that had
never been committed, but they told me that if I was really for the
Soviet power, as I said I was, I ought to confess in this affair, for the
Soviet power needed my confession; that I need have no fear of the
consequences; the Soviet regime would take into consideration my
openhearted confession and would give me the opportunity to
work and to make good my mistakes through work. At the same
time, I would have visits from my family, letters, walks, newspapers. But if I persisted in maintaining silence, I would be
subjected to pitiless repression, and not myself alone, but my wife
and children also. For months I resisted; but my situation became
so intolerable that nothing it seemed to me could be worse; in any
case I had become indifferent to everything. And I signed everything the examining judge demanded of me . . . '.

'Not Guilty', *Report of the Commission of Inquiry into charges
made against Leon Trotsky in the Moscow Trials* (1938) (London: Martin Secker and Warberg) p. 364.

(g) The style of Soviet justice (i)

Soviet justice is planned justice. The manner in which the trial is
staged and conducted, the verdict which is rendered, the sentence
which is passed, the extent to which the sentence is carried out, all
these are designed to meet whatever political objectives, internal or
external, the government may have chiefly in mind at the time.
From beginning to end, the handling of the Metrovick affair by the
Soviet authorities must be held to be governed by such considerations.

Soviet procedure in these cases is based on the confession. The
net is spread; a catch of suspects is brought in; without being
charged, they are all invited to confess, and are constrained to do so
by every device that lies to the hand of an all but all-powerful
police. Out of this medley of confessions obtained by trick or
intimidation, the case is built up and no distinction is drawn
between accused and witnesses until the case is complete and the
indictments can be framed. Often there are no witnesses properly
so called: the evidence against themselves and each other is provided by the accused themselves. In the Metrovick trial there was
only one witness who was not in the dock and he was an obvious
'agent-provocateur'.

> Lord Strang (1956) *Home and Abroad* (London: André
> Deutsch) p. 96.

(h) The style of Soviet justice (ii)

The most extraordinary part of this trial from a Western outlook is
that there should have been such a trial at all. The accused had all
entered the plea of guilty. There remained nothing for a court to do
but to hear possible pleas of clemency and to adjudge the fact and
sentence the accused. But here a so-called trial was had which lasted
for six days and in which presumably all proof was produced that
the prosecutor could possibly adduce – from our point of view an
entirely useless proceeding. There were probably two purposes for
this programme on the part of the authorities.

Off the record one is admitted to wit: that the occasion was
dramatised for propaganda purposes. It was designed: first, as a
warning to all existing and potential plotters and conspirators
within the Soviet Union; second, to discredit Trotsky abroad; and
third to solidify popular national feeling in support of the government against foreign enemies – Germany and Japan. During the
trial, every means of propaganda was employed to carry to all parts
of the country the horrors of these confessions. The newspapers
were filled not only with reports of the testimony but also
comments of the most violent character as to the accused. The
radio was also working overtime.

The other probable purpose was to disclose to the public in open
court the 'bona fides' of the confessions of the accused. Had these
confessions been made 'in chambers', or produced over the signa-
tures of the accused, their authenticity might have been denied. The
fact of the confessions could never be disputed in the face of the oral
self-accusations made in 'open court'.

70 With an interpreter at my side, I followed the testimony carefully.
Naturally, I must confess, that I was predisposed against the
credibility of the testimony of these defendants. The unanimity of
their confessions, the fact of their long imprisonment, with the
possibility of duress and coercion extending to themselves or their

75 families, all gave me grave doubts as to the reliability that could
attach to their statements. Viewed objectively, however, and based
upon my experience in the trial of cases and the application of the
tests of credibility which past experience had afforded me, I arrived
at the reluctant conclusion that the state had established its case, at

80 least to the extent of proving the existence of a widespread
conspiracy and plot among the political leaders against the Soviet
government and which under their statutes established the crimes
set forth in the indictment.

The historical background and surrounding circumstances also
85 lend credibility to the testimony. The reasoning which Sokolnikov
and Radek applied in justification of their various activities and
their hoped-for results were consistent with probability and
entirely plausible. The circumstantial detail, apparently at times
surprising even to the prosecutor, as well as to other defendants,

90 which was brought out by the various accused, gave unintended
corroboration to the gist of the charges. The manner of testifying
of various accused and their bearing on the stand also had weight
with me. The dispassionate, logical, detailed, statement of Pyatakov and the impression of despairing candour with which he gave

95 it carried conviction.

On the face of the record in this case, it would be difficult for me
to conceive of any court, in any jurisdiction, doing other than
adjudging the defendants guilty of violations of the law as set forth
in the indictment as defined by the statutes.

Davies, *op. cit.*, p. 127.

Questions

a   Why did the writer of extract (*f*) finally confess, and what did he
    confess?
★   b   Why might extract (*f*) be included in an 'inquiry into the charges
    made against Leon Trotsky in the Moscow Trials'?
c   Compare extracts (*f*) and (*g*) on the truthfulness of confessions
    in Soviet justice.
d   In extract (*g*), what is an 'agent-provocateur' (line 43)?

e What was the purpose of the show trials, according to extract (**h**)?

f Compare the views of the authors of extracts (**g**) and (**h**) as to whether Soviet justice was fair to the accused in the show trials.

2 Government

(a) Stalin's rule

Lenin, we are told, used to say: 'Here is what I think our policy should be. If anyone has suggestions to offer or can make any improvements, I am willing to listen. Otherwise, let us consider my plan adopted'. Stalin takes a different view. He is more inclined
5   to begin, if the subject under discussion concerns foreign affairs: 'I should like to hear from Molotov'. Then he might continue, 'Now what does Voroshilov think on the military aspects of this subject?' and later he would ask Kaganovich about the matter in relation to industry and transportation.
10   Gradually he will get a composite opinion from the Politburo, probably 'leading' the discussion along the lines he desires, but not appearing to lay down the law until the final conclusion is reached. Thus, superficially, at least, he seems to act as chairman of a board, or arbiter, rather than as the boss.
15   In making this distinction between the methods of Lenin and Stalin, one thing must always be remembered. Lenin knew that his Politburo was composed of potentially hostile elements, full of cabals and rivalries. Stalin and Trotsky were at loggerheads from the outset; Kamanev and Zinoviev generally played together in an
20   often shifty game and were not always to be relied upon. Rykov, Bukharin and Tomsky represented another element of discord. Lenin, therefore, found it necessary to lay down the law and take a strong line with what he once described as, 'this difficult team that I drive'.
25   In Stalin's case, his senior colleague, Molotov and Voroshilov, have been most closely associated with him as partners, friends and henchmen for more than thirty years since the old underground days in Russia, during the Revolution and Civil War, and in all the vicissitudes and conflicts that followed against enemies at home and
30   abroad. The same thing can be said of all the rest, with the only difference that some of the juniors have had a much shorter period of association with their chief. But all the Politburo members, without exception, have always been Stalin's men, throughout their careers. They were handpicked by Stalin, by virtue of his
35   commanding position as Party Secretary. Typical of the younger men are Andreyev – whom he appointed to a high post in the Secretariat at the early age of twenty-nine – and Malenkov. Well might Trotsky say, bitterly, in the hour of Stalin's first triumphs that the Dictatorship of the Proletariat had been replaced by a

40 Dictatorship of the Secretariat.

   To make a familiar comparison, the Politburo is like a first-class
football team, say Arsenal or Manchester United and Stalin is their
manager and coach. Each member of his team has his specific
position and knows what to do in any team play, but the team as a
45 whole depends upon the coach, relies upon him, and looks to him
for their leadership and inspiration – with the significant difference
that Arsenal's manager sits on the sidelines; whereas Stalin, in
addition to coaching the team, plays centre-forward as well.

   Durranty, Walter (1949) *Stalin and Co* (London: Secker and
   Warburg 1949), pp. 80–1.

Questions

a Compare the leadership styles of Lenin and Stalin as outlined in
  extract (**a**).
b Is the author of extract (**a**) supportive or critical of Stalin's style?
★ c Is this extract a fair assessment of Stalin's method of ruling?

(b) Freedoms under the Stalin Constitution

Freedom of speech, of the press, of assembly, of meetings, of street
processions is granted within the limits set in Sec. 125 para. 2 i.e.
'by placing at the disposal of the working people and their
organisations the whole press apparatus (printing shops, supplies of
5 paper) for the printing of newspapers and for the other activities
public buildings and the streets'. These qualifications suggest that
the freedoms in question are of a collective not of an individual
nature as the same words used in western democratic countries
would be understood. They are, moreover, collective in the special
10 sense that the press is entirely in the hands of the State, i.e., of the
Communist Party.

   The right to unite in public organisations includes trade unions,
co-operative associations, youth organisations, cultural, technical,
and scientific societies and the All-Union Communist Party (of
15 Bolsheviks). The latter is open not to everybody but only to the
most active and politically conscious citizens from the ranks of the
workers and other strata of the working people. The Party is
described as, 'the leading nucleus of all organisations of the
working people, both social and state'. Thus the character of the
20 other organisations in which people may unite is clearly explained;
they are organisations of the leading nucleus, which is the Party.

   As regards the guarantee of the inviolability of person, and of the
home, and secrecy of correspondence, no executive provisions
have yet been given in the Constitution. It is rather a statement of a
25 goal to be achieved later, than a complete law.

   Fruend, *op. cit.*, pp. 140–1.

(c) Party candidates

Stalin wanted – especially with the threat of foreign assault – to give
his power a broader base in the country and in this sense his
constitution was democratic. But, when setting about this, he was
copying what Lenin had done, when in exile he first built up the
30   Communist Party. In each case, the system may be described as
hand-picking. There was plenty of selection before the one candidate was chosen and in this work both party and non-party
organisations were drawn into active collaboration. The actual
slogan displayed everywhere during the election was 'The Alliance
35   of Party and Non-Party'. Where were the men or women who in a
'Stalin' or 'Bolshevik' (that is wholehearted) way would carry the
lessons and instructions of their leader far and wide into the whole
mass of the country? Where were the new fresh forces which would
rise out of the mass to put more volume into the work of the Party?
40   The Press was constantly urging the need of the most careful
scrutiny of the whole past record of each prospective candidate. It
was not unlike what we sometimes ourselves do, with a less serious
purpose; it was the good cricket coach who is constantly looking
for budding talent in the lower games.

        Pares, *op. cit.*, p. 201

(d) Party elections

45   Two features in this election will present puzzles to students of
affairs in the United States of America and in the United Kingdom.
In the first place there was only one 'Party'. In the second place – a
still more startling fact – with insignificantly few exceptions, there
was only one candidate for each vacancy. Why, then, all the
50   expensive and troublesome machinery of an election, over a
country of enormous spaces and indifferent communications: and
why the chorus of happy jubilation over the successful, almost
unanimous, return of the unopposed?
    I have written the preceding chapters in vain if I have failed to
55   convey to the reader the radical difference between the Communist
Party and any political party known to Britain or America. The
word Party applied to the former is indeed a complete misnomer.
The Communist Party is an Order of men and women vowed to
the realisation and defence of the fundamentals of the Soviet state.
60   It comes near to being a priesthood of a religion of this world. Since
there is no intention of tolerating any challenge to the fundamentals, there is also no intention of allowing any alternative order to
champion alternative principles. To find a parallel, we must
imagine a State, having not merely a National Church, but an
65   exclusive National Church, with a monopoly of spiritual influence
and authority to which no rival is tolerated by the national law. The

Communist Party in the U.S.S.R. has very few resemblances to a
political party as we understand it, but it has many resemblances to
a Church claiming universal dominion and realising that dominion
70 within national limits. In the political sense, the U.S.S.R. tolerates
no parties at all.

Maynard, John (1943) *The Russian peasant and other studies*
(London: Victor Gollancz Ltd) p. 443.

(e) Party rights

The high Party members, who now wield the power of the
Romanovs, have moved into both the palaces and the privileges of
the old aristocracy and are drinking quite as much champagne. But
75 no one can argue that they do not justify their existence by hard
and useful work for the state and by taking leadership and
responsibility. Class distinctions are rapidly springing up in Russia.
But for the present, at least, these distinctions are based on
achievement and hard work – even though the achievement may
80 sometimes be only political skill necessary to climb to the top of the
hierarchy.

'He's got everything a Commissar should have', the correspondents once said, 'a motor car, a peroxide wife with gold teeth and a
dacha'. But at least he got these things by hard work presumably,
85 (and usually), in the service of the people and the state. The
privileged class in Russia is full of the rich sap of hard work. There
is in it so far none of the rotten dead-wood of hereditary fortunes.

One of the Party's functions is to provide the Kremlin with
accurate reports on the state of Russian public opinion, for, of
90 course, this exists even as it has under Mussolini and Hitler. In the
field of foreign affairs, of course, the people have no facts other
than those provided by the government-controlled press. But in
domestic matters the Russian people have definite ideas as to what
they like and do not like. The Party is sometimes unable to check a
95 trend in public opinions. If it is a real ground-swell, they do not
fight it but divert it into proper channels.

They remember 1917, when they themselves rode to power on
the crest of a tidal wave of unrest, which the old autocracy failed to
recognise in time, and was too stupid to handle. They expect
100 similar unrest after this war, and are sure they will be quick enough
to canalise it, before it gets out of hand.

American correspondents in Russia, who are most warmly
sympathetic with the dictatorship, say that it amounts to a government by the Gallup Poll, which is much too rosy a view of the
105 facts. The dicatorship is, of course, acutely concerned with public
opinion. But most of this is created by the government's own
press; another portion may be directed into safe channels – and
there remain a few instances where the government finds it must

abandon, reverse, or postpone policies, because they are too unpopular.

> White, W. L. (1945) *Report on the Russians*, (New York: Harcourt, Brace and Co.) pp. 258–9.

Questions

a   In extract (**b**), what is meant by the phrase 'freedoms . . . are of a collective not of an individual nature' (lines 7–8)?

b   What rights do the people have, as compared to the Party, according to this extract?

c   In what sense is the Constitution democratic, according to extract (**c**)?

d   What are the differences between political parties in the West and the Communist Party in Russia, according to extract (**d**)?

e   Compare extracts (**d**) and (**e**) on the role of the Communist Party in Russia.

f   To what extent are extracts (**c**), (**d**) and (**e**) supportive of the Russian political system?

3   The personality cult

(a) Stalin as hero

His personal ascendancy is unquestionable. I was struck by the fact that, whenever his name was mentioned, it was always with a respect almost amounting to awe. The President of the Moscow Soviet was careful to impress upon me the greatness of the man in
5   the Kremlin whose vision was much wider than his. The President of the Baku Soviet was confident his plans would go through because he had the personal support of Comrade Stalin. Scarcely a speech is made without eulogistic references to 'our beloved leader Comrade Stalin'. Lenin lies in his marble mausoleum, cold in the
10   sleep of death, for wondering peasants and workers to gaze upon. But more and more, as might be expected, the personality of the living tends to overshadow that of the dead. Busts of Stalin are almost as numerous as those of Lenin. His picture is to be found everywhere.
15   I saw his face in factories, cinemas, schools, creches, on collective farms, in Soviet buildings, and in every conceivable place. Outside the house of the Trade Unions of Moscow, there was a picture of him fully twenty feet high, thrown into bold relief by the flood-lights surrounding it and gazing down at the delegates of the
20   Communist Youth International as they entered the building for their conference. It was a kindly face, yet Lenin had suggested his resignation because he was too rough in his methods.

> Citrine, *op. cit.*, pp. 324–5.

(b) Stalin and Lenin

Immediately in front of the theatre there were two white large, and beautiful, statues of Lenin and Stalin, surrounded by flags and
25 standards of the various Constituent Republics of the Soviet Union, with a background of red bunting and flowers, indirectly lighted. The facade of the old Opera House was similarly decorated, and most effective, by reason of indirect-lighting effects with four large portraits of Marx, Engels, Lenin and Stalin extending
30 across the entire front of the theatre. The interior was similarly and impressively decorated. The stage, which is at least eighty feet wide, was hung with a huge red plush draperies, as a background for still another white statue of Lenin, with a large portrait of Stalin immediately back of it – all profusely banked with flowers. A long
40 table extended across the front of the stage – at which were seated President Kalinin and a group of officials of the government. In the second tier, and immediately behind Kalinin, sat Stalin, Voroshilov and Ezhov (head of the secret police). At the opening of the meeting there was much enthusiasm and continuous applause.
45 Premier Molotov delivered an address from the speaker's dais. It was a scholarly address. The speech lasted approximately two hours. Delivery was uninspiring but met with frequent applause, particularly whenever the name 'Stalin' was mentioned. During the long discourse, it was noted that Stalin, Voroshilov and Ezhov in
50 the rear line were quite obviously whispering and joking amongst themselves.

After the intermission, there was shown a Soviet motion picture depicting Lenin and his activities for the three days immediately prior to the overthrow of the Kerensky government. The picture
55 was well done. Propaganda was, of course, omnipresent. Stalin was quite obviously dragged into the picture for several 'shots', apparently to establish that affectionate confidence existed between Lenin and Stalin.

Davies, *op. cit.*, p. 240

(c) The return of personality

In opposition to hero-worshipping historiography, to the theory
60 that history is man-made, to the writing of history round persons, Marx brought forward the economic and sociological, the materialist view of history. In that view, individuals are not much more than agents set to work by a development proceeding in accordance with its own laws. This view of history was very much in vogue in
65 the Soviet Union at first and also in the school of Pokrovsky.

The fight against Pokrovsky was a fight also for the recognition of the role of personality in history. Among the charges made against Pokrovsky was precisely that of having degraded personality

to the status of a marionette, controlled by the economic
70   process. Soon after his 'demotion' there appeared the first biog-
raphies in which personality was brought once more to the
foreground. The first of these was the novel about Peter the Great
written by Alexei Tolstoy on his return from emigration and some
articles in ideological or specialist journals re-examining the signi-
75   ficance of personality. Then, in the last ten years, the Stalin cult
became so important an element in the state and public life of the
U.S.S.R. that no further evidence need be offered here to show that
personality once more accounts for something.

Mehnert, Klaus (1952) *Stalin versus Marx*, (London: George
Allen and Unwin) p. 76.

Questions

a According to extract (*a*), why was Stalin becoming more
popular than Lenin?
b Why are there so many references to Lenin in extract (*b*)?
c Do the authors of extracts (*a*) and (*b*) appear to be in favour of
Stalin's personality cult?
d Why does the author of extract (*c*) argue against the cult of
personality?
★ *e* Using these extracts and other information known to you,
explain how the personality cult reflected Stalin's style of
government.

V Foreign Policy 1924–1941

Introduction

Russian foreign policy between the wars seemed to give out uncertain signals, as indeed it might considering its two basic – and conflicting – aims. The idea of permanent, or world, revolution had been advocated by Trotsky; but he had been defeated in the leadership contest by Stalin, not least because after revolution in Russia in 1917 there had been no further successful communist revolution in Europe, or anywhere else. Stalin had championed 'Socialism in One Country', the idea that Russia could survive on its own. However, it would be better if Russia could reduce its enemies in the short-term, at least, and the Russian foreign office, Narkomindel, spent much of its time trying to re-establish links with the west. Unfortunately Stalin could hardly jettison all Marxist theory and it was still claimed that eventually the world revolution would come about. Thus Comintern appeared to be trying to spread communism by the back door in the same countries Narkomindel was trying to link up with again. Stalin tried to play down the role of Comintern, but the west was not convinced.

This latent hostility mattered little in the 1920s when Russia was not under any real threat. But all this changed with the rise of Hitler in the early 1930s, and his avowed hatred of communism. Stalin realised that Russia could not stand on its own (especially after his purges had wrecked the armed forces) and thus he redoubled his efforts to improve links with Britain and France. Yet, for all his promises to back collective security and support Czechoslovakia in the Sudeten crisis, it was only to see the west continually fail to stand up to Hitler, while pursuing a policy of appeasement.

This approach greatly worried Stalin, always fearful of people – and countries – ganging up on him. The crux came over Germany's threat to Poland in mid-1939. Britain and France could not help Poland on their own and needed Russian assistance, but no-one fully trusted Russia, while the communists not unreasonably feared that, in the final analysis, the west would not be unhappy if Germany and Poland became friends again, and launched a joint attack on Russia. As a result of this impasse, Britain and France compromised by continuing to talk to Russia, without expecting any real breakthrough. Then the unthinkable happened; the announcement of a non-aggression pact between Russia and Germany (with a secret clause agreeing to the division of Poland between them). It was purely a marriage of convenience, with Stalin playing for time in the hope that, after Poland had fallen, Hitler would turn the way of the west. In 1940 Germany did just that, but it was not the expected long haul as in World War One; France collapsed in a bare six weeks, Stalin was aghast. He knew he was running out of time and therefore when Hitler did invade Russia in June 1941, communist rearmament was still far from complete.

1 Conflict on theories

(a) Zinoviev on how to prevent war

How can we prevent war?

The most important means for achieving this is the revolutionary enlightenment of the masses, the organisation of the masses under the leadership of the Communist Party.

5   The best issue for the whole of humanity would be if the European revolution were to come to pass before a new imperialist war broke out. Our whole policy should be directed towards this end. This would be the most economical, the most peaceful, issue (not from the pacifist but from the revolutionary point of view).

10   In any case, it is our greatest revolutionary concern to postpone war as long as possible, to try with every means in our power to prevent it. After the imperialist war which so seriously hit the industrial life of our country, peace is the most necessary condition, both for our socialist growth and for the preparation and consolida-

15   tion of the Communist Parties in other countries. The later imperialism sets war against us in motion, the stronger we will be, the Soviet Union and the world proletariat with us.

Our task is:

The building up of Socialist economy; we must build up without

20   a moment's respite, build in the teeth of all difficulties by which we are faced. We must civilise ourselves, we must work at carrying through successfully the 'cultural revolution', we must work at our own development and we must, with all our might, promote the cause of the international revolution – such is Lenin's command and

25   this command will be fulfilled.

Speech of 1925, reprinted in: Harold Fisher and Xenia Eudin *Soviet Russia and the west, 1920–27* (Stanford University Press, 1957) p. 377.

(b) A Soviet resolution 1924

Having heard the communication concerning the full 'de Jure' recognition of the U.S.S.R. by Great Britain and the establishment of full normal diplomatic relations between the two states the Second Congress of Soviets of the U.S.S.R. notes with satisfaction
30 that this historic step was one of the first acts of the first government of Great Britain representing the working classes.

The workers' and peasants' government of the U.S.S.R., which originated in the great revolution, has made the struggle for peace its foremost objective, and throughout its existence has worked
35 persistently for the re-establishment of normal relations between peoples. Unfortunately, no previous British government came to meet the government of the U.S.S.R.; as late as last May, British diplomats sent the U.S.S.R. an ultimatum, threatening to disrupt trade relations, an ultimatum pregnant with a direct threat to
40 European peace.

Throughout this period, the British working class has been the true ally of the working masses of the U.S.S.R., in their struggle for peace. The peoples of the U.S.S.R. remember the efforts of the British working masses and the advanced section of the British
45 public to end the boycott, the blockade and armed intervention. They realise that recognition was effected by the unfaltering will of the British people, who unanimously demanded it as necessary to the establishment of universal peace, to world economic reconstruction after the ruin caused by the imperialist war, and in
50 particular to Great Britain's own successful struggle against industrial stagnation and unemployment.

The Soviet government's pacific policy under the guidance of Lenin, and the loudly proclaimed determination of the British people, have at least established normal relations between the two
55 countries, relations that are worthy of the great peoples of both countries, and that lay the foundation for their friendly cooperation.

Reprinted in: *ibid*, p. 223.

(c) Stalin's foreign policy

The foreign policy of the Soviet Union is clear and explicit:

(1) We stand for peace and the strengthening of business rela-
60 tions with all countries. That is our position; and we shall adhere to this position, as long as these countries maintain like relations with the Soviet Union and as long as they make no attempt to trespass on the interests of our country.
(2) We stand for peaceful, close, and friendly relations with all
65 the neighbouring countries which have common frontiers with

the U.S.S.R. That is our position and we shall adhere to that position so long as these countries maintain like relations with the U.S.S.R. and so long as they make no attempt to trespass directly, or indirectly, on the integrity and inviolability of the
70 frontiers of the Soviet State.

(3) We stand for the support of nations which are the victims of aggression and are fighting for the independence of their country.

(4) We are not afraid of the threats of aggressors and are ready to
75 deal two blows for every blow delivered by instigators of war, who attempt to violate the Soviet borders.

The tasks of the Party in the sphere of foreign policy are:

(1) To continue the policy of peace and of strengthening business relations with all countries.
80 (2) To be cautious and not allow our country to be drawn into conflicts by warmongers, who are accustomed to have others pull the chestnuts out of the fire for them.

(3) To strengthen the might of our Red Army and Red Navy to the utmost.
85 (4) To strengthen the international bonds of friendship with the working people of all nations, who are interested in peace and friendship among nations.

> Quoted in: Pritt, D. N. (1940) *Light on Moscow* (Harmondsworth: Penguin), pp. 177–8.

(d) Comintern as no threat

Stalin reversed his peasant policy, his family policy, his foreign policy; he came out for the propaganda of Socialism by example,
90 by showing what it could do in the country under his rule. But he could not be expected to renounce his faith in ultimate revolution. As head of the Russian Communist Party – remember that is his only post in Russia – he was throughout under a crossfire from two sides – from the capitalist world in its objections to Communism
95 and from Trotsky from his alleged betrayal of it. Trotsky has even appealed in vain to the Comintern against him. Trotsky was still a big enough man to be heard everywhere; he remarked, ironically, that the Fifth and Seventh Commandments had been restored in Russia, though so far without reference to God. It was not strange,
100 therefore, if there were still signs outside of the work of Comintern established in Moscow. Meanwhile, in Russia, it was not allowed to meet for three years after Stalin's triumph; and when it reappeared, later, it was in a very purged and chastened form as an instrument for propaganda behind the line of actual, or prospec-

105   tive, enemies such as Germany's dealings with the Irish in the last
war. Its headquarters were moved away from the centre of
Moscow. It had become a side line.

        Pares, *op. cit.*, p. 221.

(e) Comintern as a threat

The struggle between the original internationalism and the natio-
nalism which has taken its place has been a long one and has been
110 fought with varying fortunes. The history of the Third International is a compendium of the struggle. It was brought into existence
because the Second International had betrayed the International
cause, by its support of national war in 1914. It began its career as
the avowed champion of World-Revolution; and it was the enthu-
115 siasm of one of its meetings which sent the Red armies to defeat
outside Warsaw. It made concession to compromise when it
dampened down the revolutionary spirit in Germany in 1923, and
further concessions in the same direction, when it endorsed the
policy of friendly alliance with the moderate parties abroad, with
120 the Kuomintang in China, with the Trade Union Congress in
Great Britain, with Pilsudski in Poland: still more when it adopted
the policy of the United Front in 1935. Its school for Asiatic and
colonial propaganda was directed against the Powers with which
the Soviet Government desired friendly relations; its extraordinary
125 plan made in 1928 for a Negro Republic in the U.S.A. was a direct
challenge. The long delays between its plenary meetings seemed to
proclaim lukewarmness or neutrality. The signature of the non-
aggression pacts including a clause against intervention in foreign
countries, on account of their internal condition; the entry into the
130 comity of nations signalised by the endorsement of the Kellogg
Plan; the acceptance of membership of the League of Nations;
appeared to repudiate subversive design. But even in 1934 the
permanent organisation of the Third International was engaged in
plans for the encouragement of revolution in three European
135 countries, one of them on terms of intimate political association
with the U.S.S.R.

        Maynard, *op. cit.*, p. 406.

Questions

  a According to extract (**a**), why did Russia need peace at that time?
★ *b* What is the 'international revolution' referred to in this extract
      (line 24)?
★ *c* In extract (**b**), what is the meaning of the phrase 'full de Jure
      recognition' (line 26–27)?
  d To which people in Britain do the Russians appeal to in this
      extract, and why?

e Do extracts (**a**), (**b**) and (**c**) show that Russia's foreign policy was essentially pacific in the early 1920s?

f According to extract (**d**), why could Stalin not completely abandon the idea of 'ultimate revolution' (line 91)?

g Compare extracts (**d**) and (**e**) on the importance of Comintern and its threat to non-communist countries.

★ h Why did Stalin largely abandon the theory of world revolution in the 1920s?

2 Co-operation

(a) A speech by Litvinov 1935

It is now universally recognised, that the danger of war hanging over Europe, and consequently over the entire world, can only be averted, or its risk reduced, to the minimum, by the collective efforts of all States, especially of the strongest. The British govern-
5 ment, by the agreement with France of 3 February, has already taken the road of the collective preservation of peace. The Soviet Government, therefore, welcomed the London agreement and promised its full co-operation. I believe that co-operation between our countries, which enclose Europe from the West and the East,
10 and merge into other continents, can have decisive importance for the preservation of peace and in your visit, Mr Eden, I am inclined to see, not merely the beginning of such co-operation, but the pledge of its continuation.

Reprinted in: Degras, *op. cit.*, p. 100.

(b) Soviet statement by Narkomindel on non-intervention in the Spanish Civil War; 23 August 1936

Referring to the conversations, which have taken place on the
15 subject of the line of conduct to be adopted in regard to the situation in Spain, I have the honour to communicate to you the following:

The government of the U.S.S.R., deploring the tragic events of which Spain is the theatre;
20 Resolved to abstain rigorously from all interference, direct or indirect, in the international affairs of that country;

Animated by the desire to avoid any complaint which might prejudice maintenance of good relations between nations,

Declares the following:
25 (1) The government of the U.S.S.R. prohibits, in so far as it is concerned, direct or indirect exportation, re-exportation and transition to a destination in Spain, the Spanish possessions, or the Spanish zone of Morocco, of all arms, munitions and

materials of war, as well as all aircraft, assembled or dismantled,
30   and all vessels of war.
(2) This prohibition applies to contracts in process of execution.
(3) The government of the U.S.S.R. will keep the other governments participating in this entente informed of all meausres taken
by it to give effect to the present declaration.
35   The government of the U.S.S.R., in so far as it is concerned, will
put this declaration into effect as soon as, in addition to the
French and British governments, who on 15 August of this
year exchanged notes on this subject, the Italian, German and
Portuguese governments shall likewise have adhered to this
40   declaration.
Reprinted in: *ibid*, pp. 203–4.

(c) The Soviet Union, the West and Non-Intervention

The Soviet Union endeavoured to remain aloof, and joined the
Non-Intervention Committee. But when it became apparent that
Germany and Italy, both of them members of the same Committee, had intervened, by military action, in favour of the insurgent
45   Franco, from the very moment of the outbreak of the Civil War, or
even before, the Soviet Union intervened in favour of the Spanish
Government, in order to prevent an easy victory by Franco's
Nationalists.
Shortly after the outbreak of the Civil War, the French Govern-
50   ment made an appeal to Italy and Great Britain for the adoption of
an agreement for non-intervention in Spain (August 1936). Britain
and France, on 15 August 1936, exchanged declarations to the effect
that Britain and France would abstain rigorously from all intervention, direct or indirect, in the internal affairs of Spain and would
55   prohibit the export, direct or indirect, or the re-export and the
transit to any destination in Spain and its possessions, or to the
Spanish force in Morocco of all arms, munitions and materials of
war, as well as all aircraft and all warships. These measures were to
be put into force as soon as Germany, Italy, the U.S.S.R., and
60   Portugal had adhered to the declaration. This was achieved during
August (Russia formally notified France of her adherence to the
declaration on 23 August).
In the meeting of the Non-Intervention Committee, Russia
declared that they could not consider themselves bound by the
65   agreement for non-intervention to any greater extent than any of
the other participants. While remaining represented on the Committee, Russia acted accordingly, when Madrid was threatened by
Franco sending weapons, planes, tanks and technical military and
political advisors to the Republicans.
70   In addition, she dispatched the International Brigade, composed
of communists from various countries, who had found an asylum

in Russia, but no Russian troops as such. Before this help was sent the Soviet government had made the fight for a democratic, (not a socialist), Spain a condition of assistance. Once established in
75 Spain, the Russians, in conformity with the United Front policy adopted by the Comintern in 1935, rejected the idea of a workers' revolution and insisted upon a strictly democratic character in the movement and endeavoured to mediate between revolting peasants and the Spanish government. They opposed the formation of
80 Soviets', expropriations, the creation of a workers' militia and terrorism against the Right. This was in line with the tactics of the Spanish Communists who were a weak party, opposed to the radicalism of the (non-Marxist) Anarcho–Syndicalists and of a Left wing of Socialists.
85 Russia withdrew from the Spanish theatre in 1938, remaining in the Non-Intervention Committee till the end of the Civil War in 1939.

Freund, *op. cit.*, pp. 520–1.

(d) A speech by Molotov, November 1938

The Soviet Union did not, and could not, take part in the bargaining of the imperialists, of the fascist and so-called demo-
90 cratic governments at the expense of Czechoslovakia. The Soviet Union did not, and could not, take part in the dismemberment of Czechoslovakia to satisfy the appetites of German fascism and its allies. No doubt can remain about Soviet policy on this point. While the French government renounced its treaty with Czechoslo-
95 vakia, at the moment of its decisive test, and came to an agreement with England and German fascism, whatever the cost to democratic Czechoslovakia, the Soviet Union showed that its attitude to international agreements is entirely different. It demonstrated to the entire world that its fidelity to the treaties it has concluded for
100 fighting the aggressor is unshakeable. Notwithstanding all the attempts, even the most scoundrelly, to portray the Soviet attitude to the Czech question as vacillating and indecisive, none, not even the most skilful, succeeded. The French and British governments sacrificed not only Czechoslovakia but their own interests as well,
105 for the sake of an agreement with the aggressors. Have they gained greater respect for their rights in the eyes of German and Italian fascism? There is no sign of it. Rather the contrary: their international authority has been considerably shaken. As you know, a division of Czechoslovak territory was made recently in Vienna
110 without their participation, Germany and Italy acting alone. But one thing is clear: the Soviet Union was not intimidated by threats from fascist countries, which cannot be said of certain so-called democratic countries. On the contrary, the Soviet Union proved to all countries its loyalty to its agreements and its readiness to fight aggression.

115   This fact is of great international importance, not only for the present moment, but for the entire future international struggle against fascism and fascist aggression. Only the Soviet Union, the land of socialism, stood and stands steadily on the basis of struggle against fascist aggression, for the defence of peace and of the
120   freedom and independence of states from fascist attack.
               Reprinted in: Degras, *op. cit.*, p. 360.

Questions

a   What reasons are given in extract (*a*) for better relations between Britain and Russia?

b   Who did Litvinov mean by his reference to the 'danger of war'?

c   To what extent does extract (*c*) explain why Russia failed to enact the promises it made in extract (*b*)?

d   Is the author of extract (*c*) supportive of the Russian actions?

★ e   How significant was Stalin's intervention in the Spanish Civil War?

★ f   Explain the reference to 'the dismemberment of Czechoslovakia' in extract (*d*) (lines 91–92)?

g   What criticisms does Molotov make of France and Britain in this extract, and why?

3 Disagreements

(a) *Western self-criticism*

It would be wearisome to multiply examples of the special attitude of Britain and other powers to the U.S.S.R. One final example will prove the point. In 1933 several British engineers in the Soviet Union were arrested and sent to trial on a charge of espionage.
5   Immediately, and while the matter was still 'sub judice', our National Government demanded their release (though one of them had actually admitted to his guilt)! When the Soviet Government refused to submit with all humility, like a small Arab chieftain, the National Government used truculent language and followed it up
10   by rushing an Act through Parliament, placing an embargo on trade with the U.S.S.R. But, on the other hand, when the Japanese Government, some four years later, arrested British subjects in China, fired on ships under the British flag and even beat up British policemen, the National Government took no such drastic action.
15   It sent a note of protest, to which the Japanese returned an apology, followed by another outrage. For this, another apology was rendered and accepted.
    How did the U.S.S.R. meet this difficult situation which they may well have regarded as one of encirclement by hostile capitalist

20   forces? One means was to strengthen the U.S.S.R. militarily, up to the point where an aggressor would think twice before launching an attack. The other means found was the conclusion of non-aggression pacts with other countries. Pacts of this kind were concluded with the smaller neighbouring countries. But, with the
25   exception of Italy, which signed a Non-Aggression Pact in 1933, the Great Powers refused to sign such pacts.

           Pritt, *op. cit.*, pp. 124–5.

(b) Soviet reply to British proposals 15 May 1939

The Soviet Government have given careful consideration to the latest proposals of the British Government, which were communicated to them on May 8, and they have come to the conclusion that
30   these proposals cannot serve as a basis for the organisation of a front of resistance against a further extension of aggression in Europe.

This conclusion is based on the following considerations:

35   (1) The English proposals do not contain principles of reciprocity with regard to the U.S.S.R. and place the latter in a position of inequality, inasmuch as they do not contemplate an obligation by Britain and France to guarantee the U.S.S.R. in the event of a direct attack on the latter by aggressors, whereas England and France, as well as Poland, enjoy such a guarantee as a result of
40   reciprocity which exists between them.

(2) The English proposals only extend a guarantee to Eastern European States bordering on the U.S.S.R., to Poland and to Romania, as a consequence of which the North Western frontier of the U.S.S.R. towards Finland, Estonia and Latvia remains
45   uncovered.

(3) On the one hand, the absence of a guarantee to the U.S.S.R. on the part of England and France, in the event of a direct attack by an aggressor, and, on the other hand, the fact that the North Western frontier of the U.S.S.R. remains uncovered, may serve
50   to provoke aggression in the direction of the Soviet Union.

The Soviet Government considers that there are at least three indispensable conditions for the creation of an effective barrier by pacific Stalin against a further extension of aggression in Europe: (i) The conclusion between Britain, France and the U.S.S.R. of an
55   effective pact of mutual assistance against aggression; (ii) The guaranteeing by these three Great Powers of States of central and eastern Europe threatened by aggression, including also, Latvia, Estonia and Finland; (iii) The conclusion of a concrete agreement between Britain, England, France and the U.S.S.R. as to the forms
60   and extent of assistance to be rendered materially to each other, and

to the guaranteed States, failing which (without such an agreement) there is a risk that, as experience of Czecho-slovakia proved, pacts of mutual assistance may be ineffective.

Reprinted in: Degras, *op. cit.*, p. 320.

(c) British counter-proposals

The British government had four objectives in view, which were to
65 prove mutually irreconcilable. These were: not to forego the chance of receiving help from the Soviet Union, in case of war; not to jeopardise the common front, by disregarding the susceptibilities of Poland and Romania; not to forfeit the sympathy of the world at large, by giving a handle to Germany's anti-Comintern pro-
70 paganda; and not to jeopardise the cause of peace by provoking violent action by Germany. Each of the Soviet three main points raised difficulties with us. As to the first, the Government throught that the conclusion of a straight pact of mutual assistance with the Soviet Union would provoke Germany and divide opinion at
75 home. As to the second, they were not yet ready to contemplate undertaking obligations towards any other of the Soviet Union's western neighbours than Poland, Romania and Turkey; and, in any event, the Soviet proposal meant that Poland and Romania were to receive Soviet assistance whether they wanted it or not. As to the
80 third it did not yet arise, but, when it did arise later, it was to prove most recalcitrant.

Strang, *op. cit.*, p. 164.

(d) Russian accusations

It is worth notice that on the 31st May, at the third session of the Supreme Soviet, Molotov said:

Certain changes in the direction of counter-acting aggression are
85 to be observed in the policy of the non-aggressive countries of Europe, too. How serious these changes are, remains to be seen. As yet, it cannot even be said whether these countries are seriously desirous of abandoning the policy of non-intervention, the policy of non-resistance to the further development of
90 aggression. May it not turn out that the present endeavour of these countries, to arrest aggression in some regions, will serve as no obstacle to the unleashing of aggression in other regions? We must, therefore, be vigilant. We stand for peace and for preventing the further development of aggression. But, we must
95 remember Comrade Stalin's precept, to be cautious and not allow our country to be drawn into conflicts by warmongers who are accustomed to have others pull the chestnuts out of the

fire for them. Only thus shall we be able to defend, to the end, the interests of our country and the interests of universal peace.

Pritt, *op. cit.*, pp. 70–1.

(e) The Nazi–Soviet pact

100 Anyway, we met for dinner at Stalin's, that Sunday, in August 1939, and, while the trophies from our hunt were being prepared for the table, Stalin told us that Ribbentrop had brought with him a draft of a friendship and non-aggression treaty which we had signed. Stalin seemed very pleased with himself. He said that when
105 the English and French, who were still in Moscow, found out about the treaty the next day, they would immediately leave for home. The English and French representatives, who came to Moscow to talk to Voroshilov, didn't really want to join forces with us against Germany at all. Our discussions with them were
110 fruitless. We knew that they weren't serious about us for an alliance and that their real goal was to incite Hitler against us. We were just as glad to see them leave.

That's how the Ribbentrop–Molotov Pact, as it was called in the west, came into being. We knew perfectly well that Hitler was
115 trying to trick us with the treaty. I heard with my own ears how Stalin said 'Of course, it's all a game to see who can fool whom. I know what Hitler's up to. He thinks he's outsmarted me, but actually it's I who have tricked him'. Stalin told Voroshilov, Beria, myself and other members of the Politburo, that, because of this
120 treaty, the war would pass us by for a while longer. Then we would see what happened.

Of course there are some people who thought that since Hitler wanted to negotiate with us he must be too frightened of us to attack. This interpretation of the treaty was very flattering to us.
125 Many people in the U.S.S.R. eagerly believed it and congratulated themselves. But we, the leaders of the government, knew better. We weren't fooling ourselves. We knew that eventually we would be drawn into the war, although, I suppose, Stalin hoped that the English and French might exhaust Hitler and foil his plan to crush
130 the west first and then turn east. This hope of Stalin's must have been part of the strategy behind our agreement to sign the treaty.

Khrushchev, *op. cit.*, pp. 150–1.

Questions

a   What criticisms of western foreign policy are made in extract (**a**)?

★ b   Why might the British be less aggressive towards Japan than towards Russia at this time?

c What criticisms of the British proposals for an alliance are made in extract (***b***)?

d Compare the British and Russian proposals in extracts (***b***) and (***c***); why did an Anglo-Russian alliance prove impossible?

e Does the English author of extract (***c***) apportion blame over the failure to reach an agreement?

f How far does extract (***d***) provide an explanation for Russia abandoning talks with Britain and France and signing a non-aggression treaty with Germany?

g Who in extract (***e***) is to blame for the failure of an Anglo-Russian alliance?

★ *h* Using this extract, and other information known to you, explain the meaning of the sentence, 'We knew that Hitler was trying to trick us with the treaty' (lines 114–15)?

4 1939–41

(a) Unexpected German successes

I remember we were all in the Kremlin together, when we heard the news over the radio, that the French army had capitulated and the Germans were in Paris. Stalin's nerves cracked when he learned about the fall of France: 'Couldn't they put up any resistance at all?'
5 he asked despairingly. Molotov and I were with him at the time.
Hitler had been stunningly successful in his conquest of Europe. He had swiftly moved his troops right up to the borders of the Soviet Union. After the fall of Poland, there was only a very tentative boundary between Hitler's forces and the Soviet Union.
10 Germany, Italy and Japan were formidable countries and they were united against us. The most pressing, and deadly, threat in all history faced the Soviet Union. We felt as though we were facing this threat all by ourselves. America was too far away to help us and, besides, it was unknown at that time how America would
15 react if the Soviet Union was attacked. And England was hanging by a thread. No one knew if the English would be able to hold out should the Hitlerites attempt an invasion across the Channel.

Khrushchev, *op. cit.*, pp. 156–7.

(b) Rumours of disagreements

Washington March 4 1941
There is considerable Soviet activity in the Balkans. Last month,
20 a report came over the Moscow radio that the Turkish–Bulgarian pact was signed through the intervention of Russia, Greece and England and the Soviet speaker said that if Germany intended marching through neutral countries, she must expect to have a

fight of it; and that Germany should not forget that there was a pact
of friendship existing between Great Britain and Turkey. Later in
the month, Tass, the official Soviet news agency, stated that the
above report, which had come through a Swiss newspaper, did not
correspond with the facts. Furthermore, a formal statement has
now been issued by the Moscow Foreign Office, that the Bulgarian
government had advised that it consented to the entry of German
troops into Bulgaria, in order to consolidate peace in the Balkans.
The Soviet Foreign Office formally notified the Bulgarian Minister, that it did not agree with the Bulgarian government as to the
correctness of the Bulgarian attitude; that this action on the part of
the Bulgarian government led not to peace, but to an extension of
the sphere of war and that the Soviet government conforming to its
peace policy would not support the Bulgarian government in the
execution of their present policy.

This is going pretty far in opposition to Hitler's plans.

Davies, *op. cit.*, p. 302.

(c) Soviet denial of disagreements: 13 June 1941

Even before the arrival of Sir Stafford Cripps, English ambassador
to the U.S.S.R., in London, but in particular after his arrival,
rumours began to appear in the English and generally in the foreign
press about the proximity of war between the Soviet Union and
Germany.

According to these rumours, first, Germany had presented to
Russia demands of a territorial and economic character and negotiations are now being conducted between Germany and the Soviet
Union for the conclusion of a new and closer agreement between
the two countries. The rumours state, secondly, that the U.S.S.R.
had rejected the demands, as a result of which Germany has begun
to concentrate troops on its frontier with the U.S.S.R., in preparation for an attack on the U.S.S.R.; and, thirdly, that the Soviet
Union, in its turn, has begun to step up preparations for war with
Germany and is also concentrating troops on its western frontiers.

Although these rumours are obviously absurd, responsible
circles in Moscow have, just the same, considered it necessary, in
view of the constant repetition of these propaganda rumours spread
by forces hostile to the Soviet Union and Germany forces interested in the further expansion and the spreading of the war, to
authorise Tass to state that they are clumsy fabrications.

Tass states that:

(1) Germany has not presented any demands to the U.S.S.R.,
nor has it asked for any new and closer agreement. Thus, there
could be no question of any negotiation on this subject.

(2) According to Soviet data, Germany, like the U.S.S.R., is

also strictly observing the stipulations of the Russo–German non-aggression pact and therefore, in the opinion of Soviet circles, rumours of Germany's intention to break the pact and open an attack on the U.S.S.R. are devoid of all foundation: the recent transfer of German troops, freed from operations in the Balkans, to the eastern and north-eastern regions of Germany is, it must be assumed, connected with other reasons, which have no bearing on Soviet–German relations.

(3) The U.S.S.R., consistently with its policy of peace, has observed, and intends to observe, the provisions of the Soviet–German non-aggression pact and, therefore, rumours that the U.S.S.R. is preparing for war with Germany are lies and provocations.

(4) The sole purpose of the summer call-up of the Red Army reserves, and of the forthcoming exercises, is the training of the reserves and the testing of the railway system which, as is known, takes place each year. To interpret these measures as hostile to Germany, is to say the least absurd.

Reprinted in: Degras, *op. cit.*, p. 489.

Questions

a According to extract (*a*), why was Stalin shocked by Hitler's military success?

b Compare extracts (*b*) and (*c*) on the evidence for disagreements between Germany and Russia.

★ c Why, in extract (*c*), might Russia deny any disagreements with Germany?

★ d Why did Russo–German relations break down in the years 1940–41?

VI The Great Patriotic War

Introduction

There is sufficient evidence to suggest that Hitler's invasion of Russia in June 1941 did not come as a surprise to Stalin; but Russia's unpreparedness did mean that the attack still came as a shock. The Germans made massive initial gains. By December 1941, Leningrad was completely surrounded and German troops had reached the suburbs of Moscow. By that date, Russia had lost 18 000 tanks and some three million troops in killed, wounded and missing; and most of those captured would never return, as fighting on the Eastern front was far more vicious than elsewhere in Europe. Hitler's sheer loathing for communist and slav meant he cared little for the rules of war and, therefore, incidentally alienated possible support from the Ukraine, and elsewhere. The Russians retaliated in kind.

Yet, despite her heavy losses and being written off by the West, Russia did survive the winter of 1941. Her great strength was her size (although Russian hagiography claimed the victory was totally due to Stalin's leadership. After his fall, it was said to be in spite of his intervention). German 'blitzkrieg' tactics worked on the basis of short but intense wars; but Russia was too big and, however much land and personnel she lost, there were always reserves of both. The Wehrmacht continued to advance in 1942, but against stiffening resistance, as Russian industry, hurriedly evacuated beyond the Urals in 1941, went into full production and started to turn out vast amounts of military equipment, including some of the best designs of the war such as the T-34 tank. Germany was halted at Stalingrad and began to retreat after Kursk. By the time the Western allies had landed in Normandy in June 1944 Germany was already in full retreat in the East; and even after D-Day Hitler maintained far more divisions in the East than in the West.

Thus Russia's contribution to the victory over Hitler was essential; and there was the rub. Stalin long suspected that the West was not pulling its weight and was quite happy to allow Russia and Germany to batter each other to a standstill, allowing Britain and the United States to then step in and pick up the spoils. Stalin demanded a Second Front from 1941 onwards. The failure to achieve one until 1944, coupled with pre-war mutual suspicion, soured East–West relations from the very start of the Great Patriotic War.

1 Russian reverses

(a) Stalin panics?

Instead of returning home that night, I waited till three o'clock to see what would happen. Sure enough, just as dawn began to break, we got word that the German artillery had opened fire. When the enemy first launched the invasion, we received orders not to shoot
5 back. Our leaders issued this strange command because they thought that, possibly, the artillery fire was a provocation on the part of some German field commander acting independently of Hitler. In other words, Stalin was so afraid of war that, even when the Germans tried to take us by surprise and wipe out our
10 resistance, Stalin convinced himself that Hitler would keep his word and wouldn't really attack us.

After the successful conclusion of our operation outside Moscow, in which we – that is the South-West Front – had taken part, I was called to Moscow to consult with Stalin. I found myself
15 confronted with a new man. He was much changed from the way he'd been at the very beginning of the war. He had pulled himself together, straightened up and was acting like a real soldier. He had also begun to think of himself as a great military strategist, which made it harder than ever to argue with him. He exhibited all the
20 strong-willed determination of a heroic leader. But I knew what sort of hero he was. I'd seen him when he had been paralysed by his fear of Hitler, like a rabbit in front of a boa constrictor. And my opinion of him hadn't changed in the meantime. During the first part of the war, when things were going badly for us, I hadn't
25 failed to notice that Stalin's signature never appeared on a single document or order. 'High Command', 'General Staff' or some other term was used, but never his name. This practice didn't change even after we repulsed the Germans outside of Moscow and Stalin began to regain his confidence. Directives continued to be
30 issued from him without his signature. And this was no accident. Nothing that Stalin ever did was an accident. Every step he ever took, good or bad, was measured carefully.

Khrushchev, *op. cit.*, pp. 192–3.

(b) Stalin as warlord

Somehow, Stalin had got word that our troops had abandoned the city of Dedovsk, northwest of Nakhabino. This was very close to

35   Moscow and he was naturally very disturbed at such unexpected intelligence, especially since on November 28 and 29, the 9th Guards Rifle Division, commanded by Major General A. P. Beloborodov, had successfully held off repeated attacks of the enemy, in the nearby region of Istra. Yet, here, twenty-four hours later, it
40   seemed that Dedovsk was in the hands of the Germans.

    Stalin called me on the telephone: 'Do you know that they've occupied Dedovsk?'

    'No, Comrade Stalin, I didn't know that.'

    The chief didn't wait to find out why I was uninformed. He
45   snapped angrily: 'A commander should know what's going on at the front!' He ordered me to proceed immediately to the spot and, 'personally organise a counterattack and retake Dedovsk'. I argued that it was not wise to leave front headquarters at such a tense moment.

50   'Never mind', Stalin said, 'We'll get along somehow. Leave Sokolovsky in charge'.

    Hanging up the phone, I quickly got hold of General Rokossovsky, of the Sixteenth Army, and asked why headquarters knew nothing about the loss of Dedovsk. He explained that the Germans
55   didn't have Dedovsk and that the place in question must be the village of Dedovo.

    It was plain that the report Stalin had received was a mistake. I decided to call Headquarters and explain the misunderstanding. But it was like trying to drive a nail into a stone. Stalin was in a
60   towering rage and demanded that I go immediately to Rokossovsky, and do everything necessary to see that this miserable village was recovered from the enemy. Moreover he demanded that I take along the Fifth Army commander, General Govorov, because, 'He is an artilleryman and he can help Rokossovksy organise artillery
65   fire to help the Sixteenth Army'.

    There was no sense in arguing. We went to see General Rokossovsky and then with him to Beloborodov's division. Beloborodov was not exactly happy to see us. He outlined the situation and made it plain that there was no tactical reason for trying to recapture the
70   houses, since they were on the far side of the ravine.

    Unfortunately, I couldn't tell him that tactical principles had nothing to do with our presence there. So, I ordered Beloborodov to send a rifle company and two tanks to drive the Germans out of the houses. it was done at dawn December 1.

    Zhukov, George (1971) *Marshall Zhukov's Greatest Battles* (London: Sphere Books Ltd) pp. 126–7.

(c) A speech by Stalin, July 3, 1941

75   What are these unfavourable factors? What are the reasons for the temporary military reverses of the Red Army?

One of the reasons for the reverses of the Red Army is the absence of a second front in Europe against the German-fascist troops. The fact of the matter is that, at the present time, there are still no armies of Great Britain, or the United States of America, on the European continent, to wage war against the German-fascist troops, with the result that the Germans are not compelled to dissipate their forces and to wage war on two fronts, in the East and in the West. Well, the effect of this is that the Germans, considering their rear in the West secure, are able to move all their troops, and the troops of their allies in Europe, against our country. The situation at present is such that our country is carrying on the war of liberation singlehanded, without any military assistance, against the combined forces of Germans, Finns, Rumanians, Italians and Hungarians. The Germans preen themselves on their temporary successes, and are lavish in the praises of their army, claiming it can always defeat the Red Army in single combat. But the Germans' claims are empty boasting, for it is incomprehensible why, in that case, the Germans have resorted to the aid of the Finns, Rumanians, Italians and Hungarians against the Red Army, which is fighting absolutely single-handedly, without any military help from outside. There is no doubt that the absence of a Second Front in Europe against the Germans considerably eases the position of the Germany army.

The other reason for the temporary reverses of the Red Army is our lack of an adequate number of tanks and, partly, of aircraft. In modern warfare, it is very difficult for infantry to fight without tanks and without adequate aircraft protection. Our aviation is superior in quality to that of the German and our valiant airmen have covered themselves with glory. But we still have fewer aircraft than the Germans. Our tanks are superior in quality to that of the German and our glorious tankmen and artillerymen have, more than once, put the vaunted troops of the Germans, with their numerous tanks to flight. But, we still have several times fewer tanks than the Germans. Therein lies the secret of the temporary success of the German armies. It cannot be said our tank-building industry is working badly and supplying our front with few tanks. NO! It is working very well and is producing quite a number of excellent tanks. But the Germans are producing considerably more tanks for they now have at their disposal, not only their own tank-building industry, but also the industry of Czechoslovakia, Belgium, Holland and France. Had it not been for this circumstance, the Red Army would long ago have smashed the German Army, which does not go into battle without tanks, and cannot stand up to the blows of our troops, if it has not got a superiority in tanks.

There is only one way of nullifying the Germans' superiority in tanks and that is by radically improving the position of our army. This way is not only to increase the output of tanks in our country

125 several times over, but also sharply to increase the production of anti-tank aircraft, anti-tank rifles and guns, anti-tank grenades and mortars, and to construct more anti-tank trenches and every other kind of anti-tank obstacle.

Herein lies our present task.

We can accomplish this task, and we must accomplish it, at all
130 costs.

> Stalin, J. V. (1945) *On the Great Patriotic War of the Soviet Union* (London: Hutchinson and Co.) pp. 14–15.

(d) A Russian explanation

On June 22, the enemy fell upon the covering forces of the Soviet Eight and Eleventh armies. The blow was unexpected and so powerful, that our troops soon lost contact with their army headquarters. The forces of the advancing enemy were too
135 sizeable for the scattered Soviet units, who could not stop the Fascists, despite bravery and coolness under fire. By the end of the first day of hostilities, elements of the enemy Fourth Panzer Group had broken through Soviet defences and were pushing forward.
140 On the first day of the war, the Baltic Military District was re-organised as the 'Northwestern Front'. It comprised twelve rifle divsions, two motorised, and four armoured divisions. These forces were inferior to Leeb's advancing army group numerically and in tanks, automatic weapons and, in particular, aircraft. The
145 enemy's principal advantage, however, was his ability to attack our units piecemeal, exploiting the fact that the main Soviet forces were far from the frontier and dispersed. Construction of fortified zones at Libau, Schauljai and elsewhere had not been completed when Hitler attacked. The solidly concentrated forces of the enemy
150 were initially engaged only by covering detachments of the North-western Front, then by motorised units, and finally by reserves, which were reaching the front line five to seven days after the start of the war, from distant peacetime locations. This deployment of our troops gave the Geman Fascist forces clear superiority in
155 strength and contributed to their victories, although they suffered high losses in the process.

Soviet operations were further complicated by the clogging of all roads with swarms of our people. Refugees from the frontier districts and more than 80 000 construction workers from the
160 fortified areas were heading towards the interior of the country. Workers, the families of soldiers, and many collective farmers had been forced to leave their homes without notice.

> Pavlov, Dmitri (1955) *Leningrad 1941* (Chicago: University of Chicago Press) p. 3.

(e) Stalin 1941

What is required to put an end to the danger imperilling our country, and what measures must be taken to smash the enemy?

165   Above all, it is essential that our people, the Soviet people, should appreciate the full immensity of the danger that threatens our country and give up all complacency, casualness and the mentality of peaceful constructive work that was so natural before the war, but which is fatal today, when war has radically changed

170   the whole situation. The enemy is cruel and implacable. He is out to seize our lands, watered by the sweat of our brows, to seize our grain and oil, secured by the labour of our hands. He is out to restore the rule of the landlords, to restore tsarism, to destroy the national culture and the national existence as States of the Russians:

175   Ukrainians, Byelorussians, Lithuanians, Latvians, Estonians, Uzbeks, Tatars, Moldavians, Georgians, Armenians, Azerbaijanians and the other free people of the Soviet Union, to Germanise them, to turn them into the slaves of German princes and barons. Thus the issue is one of life and death for the Soviet State, of life

180   and death for the peoples of the U.S.S.R.; the issue is whether the peoples of the Soviet Union shall be free, or fall into slavery. The Soviet people must realise this and abandon all complacency; they must mobilise themselves and reorganise all their work on a new wartime footing, where there can be no mercy to the enemy.

185   Further, there must be no room in our ranks for whimperers and cowards, for panic-mongers and deserters; our people must know no fear in the fight and must selflessly join our patriotic war of liberation against the fascist enslaver.

Stalin, *Great Patriotic War*, p. 25.

Questions

a   Compare the criticisms of Stalin's wartime leadership in extracts (**a**) and (**b**).

★   b   Why do you think the authors of these two extracts were so critical of Stalin?

c   What reasons does Stalin give in extract (**c**) for the present reverses suffered by the Russian army?

d   How pessimistic is Stalin's reading of the situation in this extract?

e   Who is to blame for the initial reverses according to extract (**d**)?

f   Who does Stalin appeal to in extract (**e**), and in what ways is this a change of policy?

★   g   Using these extracts, and other information known to you, explain why the German armed forces were so successful in the initial stages of their invasion of Russia.

2 Conditions for victory

(a) The siege of Leningrad

Life was especially hard for children who had just turned twelve. At twelve a 'dependent's' ration card replaced the 'child's' card which had been good until then. His food ration was cut just as the child was growing adult enough to take active part in the work of
5 disarming incendiary bombs, and to bear on his weak shoulders some of the heavy work and responsibility of his home. Parents sometimes denied themselves bread to support the enfeebled bodies of their children, but in the process did severe harm to their own bodies.

10   Cold had settled down to stay in the unheated apartments of the city. Remorselessly, it froze the exhausted people. Dystrophy and cold sent 11 085 people to their graves during November, the first to fall under death's scythe being the old men. Their bodies, in contrast to those of women of the same age, or young men, offered
15 no resistance to acute hunger.

Death overtook people everywhere. As he walked along the street, a man might fall and not get up. People would go to bed at home and not rise again. Often death would come suddenly, as men worked at their machines.

20   Since public transport was not operating, burial was a special problem. The dead were usually carried on sledges, without coffins. Two or three relatives or close friends would haul the sledge along the seemingly endless streets, often losing strength and abandoning the deceased halfway to the cematary, leaving to
25 the authorities the task of disposing of the body. Employees of the municipal public services and health service cruised the streets and alleys to pick up the bodies, loading them onto trucks. Frozen bodies, drifted over with snow, lined the cemeteries and their approaches. There was not enough strength to dig into the deeply
30 frozen earth. Civil defence crews would blast the ground to make mass graves, into which they would lay tens, and sometimes hundreds, of bodies, without even knowing the names of those they buried.

May the dead forgive the living who could not under those
35 desperate conditions perform the last ceremonies due honest laborious lives.

        Pavlov, *op. cit.*, pp. 122–3.

(b) Russian behaviour

Stalin interrupted: 'Yes, you have of course read Dostoevsky? Do you see what a complicated thing is man's soul, man's psyche? Well, then, imagine a man who has fought from Stalingrad to
40 Belgrade – over thousands of kilometers of his own devastated

land, across the dead bodies of his comrades and dearest ones. How can such a man react normally? And what is so awful in his having fun with a woman after such horrors? You have imagined the Red Army to be ideal. And it is not ideal, nor can it be, even if it did not
45 contain a certain percentage of criminals – we opened up our prisons and stuck everybody in the army. There was an interesting case. An Air Force Major had fun with a woman and a chivalrous engineer appeared to protect her. The Major drew a gun: 'Eh you mole from the rear! – and he killed the engineer. They sentenced
50 the Major to death. But somehow the matter was brought before me and I made enquiries – I have the right as commander in chief in time of war – and I released the Major and sent him to the front. Now he is one of our heroes. One has to understand the soldier. The Red Army is not ideal. The important thing is that it fights
55 Germans – and it is fighting them well while the rest doesn't matter.'

> Djilas, Miloran (1962) *Conversations with Stalin* (Orlando: Harcourt Brace) pp. 110–11.

(c) German behaviour

When the Germans came back in 1941, they not only brought in priests, but many other tame Ukrainians and again set up a separatist movement, recruiting a Ukrainian militia for which
60 they found a fairly ample supply of anti-Russian or anti-Soviet Quislings.

The Germans came to every village with recruiting appeals for their labour service in the Reich. It was supposed not to be compulsory, but, if enough likely candidates did not volunteer, the
65 Quisling Cossacks would then come around and see that they did.

Towards the end of the occupation, the people came to dislike the Quisling Cossacks more than they did the Germans. Then the Quislings presently fell out with the Germans, with the result that in some areas the Quislings were fighting both the Wehrmacht and
70 the Red Army.

But out of all this confusion emerges the fact that a majority of the Ukrainians were loyal to the Soviet Union throughout – how large a majority is anybody's guess.

There is no doubt, however, that most Ukrainians hated the
75 Germans. During their Ukrainian trip, the reporters visited a village near Uman which had been liberated so recently that two burned German trucks were still smouldering in a ditch and the Foreign Office had had no time to organise propaganda, even if it were disposed to.

80 There they talked to two girls who said the Germans had mobilised them for 'voluntary' labour service. They were loaded onto trains and spent weeks being shunted around until they

arrived in a big labour dispersal camp. In adjoining pens the
85 Germans kept British and Russian prisoners of war. The girls said
that if it hadn't been for the pieces of chocolate and biscuit from
Red Cross parcels, which the British and French threw over the
fence to them, the Russian civilians would have starved. Finally,
the British war prisoners started so strong an agitation that the
90 Germans relented and provided the Russians with food up to the
British standard. The two girls had got away ingeniously. One of
them stuck her hand in a loom and the other poisoned herself with
nicotine tea from cigarette butts. So, the Germans, declaring them
unfit for work, sent them home.
95   In the same Ukrainian village, the girls led them to a
house where a woman and her three children lay dead on the floor,
their blood not yet dry from the bayonets of the departing
Germans.

> White, *op. cit.*, pp. 172–3.

Questions

a What is the purpose of extract (**a**)?
b How is Stalin portrayed in extract (**b**)?
c In extract (**c**), what was a Quisling (line 61)?
d To what extent do extracts (**a**) and (**c**) explain Stalin's attitude as
   set out in extract (**b**)?

(d) Hitler's mistakes

Hitler's unusually vivid powers of imagination led him to under-
estimate the known strength of the Soviet Union. He maintained
that mechanisation on land and in the the air offered fresh chances
of success, so that comparisons with the campaigns of Charles XII
5 of Sweden, or Napoleon, were no longer relevant. He maintained
that he could rely, with certainty, on the collapse of the Soviet system,
as soon as his first blows reached their mark. He believed the
Russian populace would embrace his National–Socialist ideology.
But as soon as the campaign began, almost everything was done to
10 prevent any such thing from taking place. By ill-treating the native
populations in the occupied Russian territories that were administered by high Party functionaries, and by reason of his decision to
dissolve the Russian state and to incorporate considerable areas into
Germany, Hitler succeeded in uniting all Russians under the banner
15 of Stalin. They were now fighting for Holy Mother Russia and
against a foreign invader.

> Guderian, Heinz (1952) *Panzer Leader*, (London: Michael
> Joseph) p. 440.

(e) *Western assistance*

The war's climax came in in 1943, with the successful defence of
Stalingrad. The Germans had, by this time, been dealt a crippling
blow to their air force in the great battles with the British in North
20   Africa. Russians point out scornfully that this African campaign
involved few men; however, it required masses of highly complicated transport and machines.

Furthermore, the RAF and the Eighth Air Force in England were
by then pounding German industry, and the Germans had to strip
25   the Russian front of fighters, to defend their home factories, so that
for the first time the Russians had superiority in the air. Lend-lease,
including thousands of trucks, was now pouring in, the German
lines of communication were perilously extended and, for the first
time, it was possible for a Russian army to move quickly out to
30   envelop and cut off a German army, as theirs had been enveloped
so many times before.

After that, Germany's superiority in weapons was slowly reduced by Allied air poundings, while Russia's supply increased.
Her own factories behind the Urals were working; new ones were
35   equipped with American machine tools. By the summer of 1944 at
least half of the Red Army's road transportation was being supplied
by 210 000 American military trucks, 40 000 jeeps and 30 000 other
military motor vehicles. She also had 5600 American tanks and
tank destroyers. At last, Russia's crushing superiority in man
40   power could become effective.

White, *op. cit.*, pp. 124–5.

(f) *Russian success*

In the name of the liberation of our country from the hated enemy,
in the name of final victory over the German fascist invaders – I
order:

(1) Indefatigably to perfect military training and to strengthen
45   discipline, order and organisation throughout the Red Army and
Navy.
(2) To deal stronger blows against the enemy troops, to pursue the
enemy indefatigably and persistently, without allowing him to
consolidate himself on defence lines. To give him no respite by day
50   or night, to cut his communications, to surround his troops and
annihilate them, if they refuse to lay down their arms.
(3) To fan brighter the flames of guerrilla warfare in the rear of the
enemy, to destroy the enemy's communications, to blow up
railway bridges, to frustrate the transport of enemy troops and the
55   supply of arms and ammunition, to blow up and set fire to army
stores, to attack enemy garrisons, to prevent the retreating enemy

from burning down our villages and towns, to help the advancing Red Army, heart and soul, and by all possible means.

In this lies the guarantee of our victory.
> Stalin's Order of the Day, 23 February 1943, reprinted in Stalin, *Great Patriotic War* p. 46.

Questions

a What mistakes did Hitler make according to extract (*d*)?
b To whom does extract (*e*) analyse the final victory in Russia and why?
c How will Russia win the war, according to extract (*f*)?
★ d Do extracts (*d*), (*e*) and (*f*) give a sufficient explanation for the eventual defeat of Germany by Russia?

3 Allied relations

(a) Churchill on Russia

The Nazi regime is indistinguishable from the worst features of Communism. It is devoid of all theme and principle, except appetite and racial domination. It excels all forms of human wickedness in the efficiency of its cruelty and ferocious aggression.
5 No one has been a more consistent opponent of Communism than I have for the last twenty-five years. I will unsay no word that I have spoken about it. But all this fades away before the spectacle which is now unfolding. The past, with its crimes, its follies, and its tragedies, flashes away. I see the Russian soldiers standing on the
10 threshold of their native land, guarding the fields which their fathers have tilled since time immemorial. I see them guarding their homes, where mothers and wives pray – ah yes for there are times when we all pray – for the safety of their loved ones, the return of the breadwinner, of their champion, of their protector. I see the ten
15 thousand villages of Russia, where the means of existence was wrung so hardly from the soil, but where there are still basic human joys, where maidens laugh and children play. I see advancing upon this, in hideous onslaught, the Nazi war machine with its clanking heel-clicking officers, its crafty expert agents, fresh from
20 the cowing and tying down of a dozen countries.
> Speech of 21 June 1941 reprinted in: Winston S. Churchill, *The Unrelenting Struggle*, (London: Cassell 1946) p. 178.

(b) A communist on Stalin

Stalin turned to relations with the Western allies from another aspect and continued: 'Perhaps you think that just because we are

the allies of the English, that we have forgotten who they are and
who Churchill is? They find nothing sweeter than to trick their
25 allies. During the First World War, they constantly tricked the
Russians and the French. And Churchill? Churchill is the kind who
if you do not watch him will slip a Kopeck out of your pocket. And
Roosevelt? Roosevelt is not like that. He dips in his hand only for
bigger coins. But Churchill? Churchill – even for a Kopeck.'
    Djilas, *op. cit.*, p. 73.

(c) *Stalin to Churchill*

30 M. Stalin to the Prime Minister   18 July 1941
    Let me express my gratitude for the two personal messages
which you have addressed to me.
    Your messages were the starting-point of developments which
subsequently resulted in agreement between our two governments.
35 Now, as you said with full justification, the Soviet Union and
Great Britian have become fighting allies in the struggle against
Hitlerite Germany. I have no doubt that, in spite of the difficulties,
our two States will be strong enough to crush our common enemy.
    Perhaps it is not out of place to mention that the position of the
40 Soviet Union forces at the front remains tense. The consequences
of the unexpected breach of the Non-Aggression Pact by Hitler, as
well as of the sudden attack against the Soviet Union – both facts
bringing advantages to the German troops – still remain to be felt
by the Soviet armies.
45   It seems to me, therefore, that the military situation of the Soviet
Union, as well as of Great Britain, would be considerably improved if there could be established a front against Hitler in the
West – Northern France – and in the North – the Arctic.
    A front in Northern France could not only divert Hitler's forces
50 from the East, but, at the same time, would make it impossible for
Hitler to invade Great Britain. The establishment of the front just
mentioned would be popular with the British army, as well as with
the whole population of Southern England.
    I fully realise the difficulties involved in the establishment of such
55 a front. I believe, however, that in spite of the difficulties it should
be formed not only in the interests of our common cause, but also
in the interests of Great Britain herself. This is the most propitious
moment for the establishment of such a front, because now Hitler's
forces are diverted to the East and he has not yet had the chance to
60 consolidate the position occupied by him in the West.
        Reprinted in: Winston S. Churchill, *The Second World War*,
        Volume 3: The Grand Alliance, (London: Cassell 1956),
        pp. 309–10.

(d) *Churchill to Stalin*

Prime Minister to Monsieur Stalin   20 July 1941
    I am very glad to get your message and to learn from many sources of the valiant fight and many vigorous counter-attacks with which the Russian armies are defending their native soil. I fully
65 realise the military advantage you have gained by forcing the enemy to deploy and engage on a forward westerly front, thus exhausting some of the force of his initial effort.
    Anything sensible and effective that we can do to help will be done. I beg you, however, to realise limitations imposed upon us
70 by our resources and geographical position. From the first day of the German attack upon Russia, we have examined possibilities of attacking Occupied France and the Low Countries. The Chiefs of Staff do not see any way of doing anything on a scale likely to be of the slightest use to you. The Germans have forty divisions in
75 France alone, and the whole coast has been fortified by German diligence for more than a year and bristles with cannon, wire, pill-boxes and beach-mines. The only part where we could have even temporary air superiority and air fighter protection is from Dunk-irk to Boulogne. This is one mass of fortifications, with scores of
80 heavy guns commanding the sea approaches, many of which can fire right across the Straits. To attempt a landing in force would be to encounter a bloody repulse and petty raids would only lead to fiascos doing far more harm than good to both of us. It would be all over without their having to move, or before they could move a
85 single unit from your front.
    You must remember that we have been fighting alone for over a year and that, though our resources are growing and will grow fast from now on, we are at the utmost strain, both at home and in the Middle East, by land and air, and also that the Battle of the
90 Atlantic, on which our life depends, and the movement of all our convoys in the teeth of U-boat and Focke-Wulf blockade strains our naval resources, great though they may be, to the utmost limit.
    It is, therefore, to the North we must look for any speedy help
95 we can give. The Naval Staff have been preparing for three weeks past an operation by seaborne aircraft upon German shipping in the north of Norway and Finland, hoping thereby to destroy enemy power of transporting troops by sea to attack your Arctic flank. We have asked your Staffs to keep a certain area clear of
100 Russian vessels between July 28 and August 2, when we shall hope to strike. Secondly, we are sending forthwith some cruisers and destroyers to Spitzbergen, whence they will be able to raid enemy shipping in concert with your own forces. Thirdly, we are sending a flotilla of submarines to intercept German traffic on the Arctic
105 coast, although owing to perpetual daylight, this service is particu-

larly dangerous. Fourthly, we are sending a minelayer with various supplies to Archangel.

This is the most we can do at the present. I wish it were more. Pray let the utmost secrecy be kept until the moment when we tell you publicity will not be harmful.

Reprinted in *ibid*, p. 311.

Questions

a In extract (*a*), how does Churchill defend the idea that Britain should now assist Russia?

b Compare extracts (*a*) and (*b*) with regard to each writer's attitude towards the other's country.

★ c Using these extracts, and other information known to you, explain why, in June 1941, Stalin and Churchill did not trust each other.

d Compare the arguments for and against a second front, as outlined in extracts (*c*) and (*d*). How valid are they?

VII   World War to Cold War

Introduction

It did not take long, once Russia had been invaded, for the allies to discover that they had little in common, other than the fact that they were all at war with Germany, the accession of the USA to the allied side in December 1941, notwithstanding. This is not to deny that the 'Big Three' could co-operate; whatever their disagreements, they were all determined to defeat Germany and her allies and did, at least, hold meetings. The axis powers were a far less cohesive force. Within days of Hitler's invasion of Russia, Stalin and Churchill were communicating by letter. A first meeting took place in Moscow in December 1941. By the end of the war, the leaders of Great Britain, the USA and Russia had already met together twice at Teheran and Yalta and were poised for a third meeting, in the ruins of Hitler's Germany, at Potsdam. From the very start, and even when the war was at its most desperate, the talk was not only of tactics (which chiefly consisted of Stalin demanding a second front and the others, Britain in particular, arguing for a postponement) but what to do, once Germany was defeated.

All three powers agreed that another such war should not happen again. For the west this meant, predominantly, that Germany should be treated in a way that removed her capacity to be a military threat. Stalin wanted to go further: Germany must be sufficiently weakened as to never be a threat again and East Europe must be dependable and friendly towards Russia. Here one must take into account recent history. By 1945 the Soviet Union had lost 20 million citizens, the bulk of them civilians, in what had been the third major invasion of Russia in under 40 years. Neither Britain nor the USA had been invaded; the latter had not even been bombed. Such vastly different backgrounds meant very different approaches after the war. The West saw Stalin's demands as proof that he wanted to expand the Russian Empire. Traditional suspicion of communism reappeared: indeed, it was the West that suggested Germany be divided into zones, rather than all powers having a joint control, in order to keep Russian influence away from the Ruhr. Mutual suspicion encouraged both sides to more extreme positions. Fearful of Western influence, in the form of economic help, and anti-Soviet feeling, Stalin took a firm hold on Eastern Europe. Distrusting Russian intentions, the Western powers united their German zones and initiated a new currency, in West Germany alone. The subsequent Berlin blockade and airlift became one of the first signs of that curious mixture of peaceful hostility that was to become known as the Cold War.

1 Wartime meetings

(a) A Foreign Office view

Stalin said our work on drafts was interesting, but what really interested him was Russia's future frontiers. He wants us, here and now, to recognise Russia's 1941 frontiers, i.e. including bits of Finland, Baltic States and Bessarabia. We told him we couldn't do
5 this and he had given no warning of this requirement to us. Argued, inconclusively, till 3 a.m., and then left without anything settled.

Difficult to say whether Stalin is impressive. There he is – a greater dictator than any Tsar – and more successful than most. But
10 if one didn't know that, I don't know that one would pick him out of a crowd. With his little twinkly eyes and his stiff hair brushed back he is rather like a porcupine. Very restrained and quiet. Probably a sense of humour. I thought at first he was simply bluffing. But I was wrong.

Dilks, David (ed.) (1971) *The Diaries of Sir Alexander Cadogan* (London: Cassell) p. 422

(b) Churchill on Stalin

15 At my first conversation with M. Stalin and M. Molotov on December 16 M. Stalin set out in some detail what he considered should be the postwar territorial frontiers in Europe, and in particular his ideas regarding the treatment of Germany. He proposed the restoration of Austria as an independent State, the
20 detachment of the Rhineland from Prussia as an independent State or a protectorate and possibly the constitution of an independent State of Bavaria. He also proposed that East Prussia should be transferred to Poland and the Sudetenland returned to Czechoslovakia. In general the occupied countries, including Czechoslovakia
25 and Greece, should be restored to their prewar frontiers, and M. Stalin was prepared to support any special arrangements for securing bases etc, for the United Kingdom in Western European countries – e.g. France, Belgium, the Netherlands, Norway and Denmark. As regards the special interests of the Soviet Union, M.

30   Stalin desired the restoration of the position in 1941, prior to the
      German attack, in respect of the Baltic States, Finland and Bessar-
      abia. The Curzon Line should form the basis for the future Soviet–
      Polish frontier, and Roumania should give special facilities for
      bases etc, to the Soviet Union, receiving compensation from
35   territory now occupied by Hungary.
         In the course of this first conversation, M. Stalin generally agreed
      with the principle of restitution in kind by Germany to the
      occupied countries, more particularly in regard to machine tools,
      etc, and ruled out money reparations as undesirable. He showed
40   interest in a postwar military alliance between the democratic
      countries and stated that the Soviet Union had no objection to
      certain countries of Europe entering into a federal relationship, if
      they so desired.
         In the second conversation, on December 17, M. Stalin pressed
45   for the immediate recognition by His Majesty's Government of the
      future frontiers of the U.S.S.R. more particularly in regard to the
      inclusion within the U.S.S.R. of the Baltic States and the restora-
      tion of the 1941 Finnish–Soviet frontier. He made the conclusion of
      any Anglo–Soviet agreement dependent upon agreement on this
50   point. I, for my part, explained to M. Stalin that in view of our
      prior undertakings to the United States Government it was quite
      impossible for His Majesty's Government to commit themselves at
      this stage to any postwar frontiers in Europe, although I undertook
      to consult His Majesty's Government in the United Kingdom, the
55   United States Government and His Majesty's Government in the
      Dominions on my return.

>   Churchill, Winston S. (1956) *The Second World War*,
>   Volume 3: The Grand Alliance (London: Cassell)
>   pp. 92–3.

Questions

a   How flexible a negotiator does Stalin appear to be, according to
    extracts (**a**) and (**b**)?
★ b   Why does Stalin put forward these particular claims, as outlined
    in these two extracts?
c   To what extent does Churchill agree with Stalin's demands in
    extract (**b**)?

(c) Teheran

THE PRIME MINISTER said that it would be a great help if
round the very table we could learn what were the Russian ideas
about the frontiers. He would then be glad to put the matter before
the Poles and to say frankly that he thought the conditions fair. His
5   Majesty's Government would be prepared to tell the Poles that the

plan was a good one and the best that they were likely to get, and
that His Majesty's Government would not argue against the Soviet
Government at the peace table. Then we could get on with the
President's idea of resuming relations. What we wanted was a
10 strong and independent Poland, friendly to Russia.

MARSHAL STALIN said that this was true, but that the Poles
could not be allowed to seize the Ukraine and White Russian
territory. That was not fair. According to the 1939 frontier the soil
of the Ukraine and White Russia was returned to the Ukraine and
15 White Russia. Soviet Russia adhered to the frontiers of 1939, for
they appeared to be enthnologically the right ones.

MR EDEN asked if this meant the Ribbentrop–Molotov line.

MARSHAL STALIN said, Call it whatever you like.

M. MOLOTOV remarked that it was generally called the
20 Curzon Line.

Churchill then produced a map, on which were marked both the
Curzon Line and the 1939 Polish–Soviet border, and he indicated
on it the line of the Oder. The discussion then focused on the city of
Lvov, with Eden suggesting that under Lord Curzon's line, Lvov
25 was intended to be inside the Polish frontier. Stalin disagreed.
Churchill's map, he said, had not been drawn right. Lvov should
be left on the Russian side. The line should go westward of Lvov,
towards the town of Przemysl.

Gilbert, Martin (1986) *Road to Victory, Churchill 1941–45*
(London: Heinemann) pp. 588–9.

(d) Yalta

After a brief adjournment Stalin spoke. He said that he understood
30 the British Government's feeling that Poland was a question of
honour but for Russia it was both a question of honour and
security; of honour because the Russians had had many conflicts
with the Poles and the Soviet Government wished to eliminate the
causes of such conflicts; of security, not only because Poland was
35 on the frontiers of Russia but because throughout history Poland
had been a corridor through which Russia's enemies had passed to
attack her. During the last thirty years the Germans had twice
passed through Poland. They passed through because Poland was
weak. Russia wanted to see a strong and powerful Poland, so that
40 she would be able to shut this corridor of her own strength. Russia
could not keep it shut from the outside. It could only be shut from
the inside by Poland itself, and it was for this reason that Poland
must be free, independent and powerful. This was a matter of life
and death for the Soviet State. Their policy differed greatly from
45 that of the Tsarist Government. The Tsars had wanted to oppress
and assimilate Poland. Soviet Russia had started a policy of
friendship, and friendship moreover with an independent Poland.

That was the whole basis of the Soviet attitude, namely, that they wanted to see Poland independent, free and strong.

50 He then dealt with some of the problems which Mr. Roosevelt and I had put forward. The President, he said, had suggested there should be some modification of the Curzon Line and that Lvov and perhaps certain other districts should be given to Poland and I had said that this would be a gesture of magnanimity. But the Curzon
55 Line had not been invented by the Russians. It had been drawn up by Curzon and Clemenceau and representatives of the United States at the conference in 1918, to which Russia had not been invited. The Curzon Line had been accepted against the will of Russia on the basis of ethnographical data. Lenin had not agreed
60 with it. He had not wished to see the town and district of Bialystok given to Poland. The Russians had already retired from Lenin's position, and now some people wanted Russia to take less than Curzon and Clemenceau had conceded. That would be shameful. When the Ukrainians came to Moscow they would say Stalin and
65 Molotov were less trustworhy defenders of Russia than Curzon and Clemenceau. It was better that the war should continue a little longer, although it would cost Russia much blood, so that Poland could be compensated at Germany's expense.

Chuchill, *op. cit.*, vol. 6 *Triumph and Tragedy* pp. 304–5.

(e) A British overview

Of Teheran and Yalta fifteen months later there has been and there
70 will be much criticism. But two things always need to be born in mind in fairness to the part played at both conferences by Churchill and Roosevelt. The first was the supreme importance to the Allied cause of ensuring that the Soviet Union continued to throw all its energy and resource into the struggle. Constantly the Western
75 Powers were made aware of suspicions that found easy lodgement in the Russian mind, and one of the major anxieties in the minds of the Western Governments, as perhaps it was in the mind of the Soviet, was the possibility of the other making a separate peace. The second was that at the time no one could have the least idea of
80 what it would demand in life and time to win victory over Japan. Both on the Chinese mainland and on the homelands of Japan, it was to be expected that we should meet with opposition, stubborn and unyielding. The possibilities of the atom bomb were not yet proved and it might mean much to secure the co-operation of the
85 Soviet in this area.

Earl of Halifax (1957) *Fullness of Days*, (London: Collins) p. 289.

Questions

★ a Why, in extract (c) might the Russians object to the phrase, Ribbentrop–Molotov line (line 17)?

b Compare the Russian demands concerning Poland in extracts
    (*c*) and (*d*).
c Do extracts (*c*) and (*d*) give any suggestion of disagreement
    between Russia and the West?
d To what extent does extract (*e*) provide an explanation for the
    conciliatory approach adopted by the West in extracts (*c*) and
    (*d*)?

2 Cold War

(a) Stalin and the Cold War

It was certainly Stalin's conviction that the postwar conflict was
neither avoidable nor reversible. This view was articulated in his
speech of February 9, 1946, delivered just prior to the nationwide
elections for the Supreme Soviet. An authoritative statement of the
5   Soviet world view, the speech sets forth Stalin's interpretation of
the nature and meaning of the Second World War, his justification
for policies pursued before and during the conflict, and prescrip-
tions for the future. If contemporary observers had failed to discern
from the massive purges of the 1930s or from the collectivisation
10 horrors what Stalin's true intentions and methods were, then this
speech and events that would soon transpire should have cleared
away any uncertainties.

If there was any doubt of his regime's continuing commitment to
a Marxist–Leninist world view, it should have been dispelled in
15 Stalin's analysis of the causes of the war. He described it as the
'inevitable result of the development of world economic and
political forces on the basis of modern monopoly capitalism,' and
in particular of 'the law of uneven development' of capitalism. As
such the war was an unavoidable and inevitable consequence of
20 capitalism, and it was also not unlikely that such a struggle should
again occur.

How, then, had the Soviet Union found itself enmeshed in a
struggle between two hostile camps of the capitalist world? Soviet
participation, Stalin said, was founded upon and enhanced 'the
25 anti-fascist and liberation character' of the war. It was on this basis
and no other that the great coalition among the United States,
Great Britain and the U.S.S.R. had been created. Although this
argument totally ignores the fact that in 1939 the Soviet Union had
broken away from the anti-fascist struggle and pursued a tactical
30 alliance with Hitler, Stalin's concern was less to provide his
listeners with a complete history than to demonstrate to them the
very limited purposes for which the Soviets had made common
cause with the Western allies.

Much can be learned from the manner in which Stalin adduced
35 the reasons for, and meaning of, the Soviet victory in the war. First

of all, it meant the triumph of the 'Soviet social order' – by test of fire it had proved its unquestionable vitality and its superiority to any non-Soviet form of social organisation. Secondly, victory had proved the viability of the 'multinational' Soviet state system. 40 Third, and clearly last, the Soviet triumph had showed the heroic character of the Soviet Army.

Nogee, Joseph and Donaldson, Robert (1981) *Soviet Foreign Policy since World War Two* (New York: Peregrine Press) p. 57.

(b) A speech by Anthony Eden, February 26, 1946

If I may, I want to try to look at the causes of this unease and make one or two suggestions which might help to remove them. Let me start with what, I think, troubles us most of all – the present state of 45 Anglo–Soviet relations. It has been said many times that it is difficult for us to understand the profound impression that has been made upon the minds of the Soviet government and the Soviet people by the wide and deep invasion of their land by the German armies and by the distress and suffering that accompanied the 50 event. That is perfectly true, and it is perhaps difficult for an island people entirely to understand it because, despite the fact that modern inventions have resulted in our being militarily no longer an island, it is, none the less, true that our mental approach to this question is still the mental approach of an island people.

55 I am convinced that it is the scourge of that invasion – and not the only one in that country – which is the dominant motive in Soviet foreign policy. It does not excuse some things which I shall talk about in a moment, but it is there. Coupled with it is the memory that it was only 80,000,000 Germans who nearly dealt a mortal 60 thrust to 180,000,000 Russians and a determination that so far as it lies in the power of the Union, Germany shall not be in a position to do so again. That, I think, is the second dominant note of Soviet foreign policy. I say those things, not to excuse, but that so we may try, in fairness, to set out the position, as it seems to be. The 65 determination not to allow Germany to be in a position ever to do this again and this alarm – I think that is the right word – which the near approach of the Germans to Moscow created, have resulted in Soviet determination to have as friendly neighbours as they can. And there, almost at once, their policy results in difficulties and 70 complications for the Soviet Government's allies.

It often happens that those whom the Soviet Government think they can trust among their neighbours are not those whom the majority in those countries wish to govern them. That is undoubtedly true.

Reprinted in: Anthony Eden, *Freedom and Order: Selected Speeches, 1939–46*, (London: Faber and Faber 1947) pp. 385–6.

(c) The Truman Doctrine

75 One of the primary objectives of the foreign policy of the United
States is the creation of conditions in which we and other nations
will be able to work out a way of life free from coercion. This was a
fundamental issue in the war with Germany and Japan. Our victory
was won over countries which sought to impose their will, and
80 their way of life, upon other nations.

To ensure the peaceful development of nations, free from
coercion, the United States has taken a leading part in establishing
the United Nations. The United Nations is designed to make
possible lasting freedom and independence for all its members. We
85 shall not realise our objectives, however, unless we are willing to
help free peoples to maintain their free institutions and their
national integrity against aggressive movements that seek to impose on them totalitarian regimes. This is no more than a frank
recognition that totalitarian regimes imposed on free people, by
90 direct or indirect aggression, undermine the foundations of international peace and hence the security of the United States.

The peoples of a number of countries of the world have recently
had totalitarian regimes forced upon them against their will. The
government of the United States has made frequent protests against
95 coercion and intimidation, in violation of the Yalta Agreements, in
Poland, Rumania and Bulgaria. I must also state that in a number of
other countries there have been similar developments.

At the present moment in world history nearly every nation
must choose between alternative ways of life. The choice is too
100 often not a free one.

One way of life is based upon the will of the majority, and is
distinguished by free institutions, representative government, free
elections, guarantees of individual liberty, freedom of speech and
religion, and freedom from political oppression.
105 The second way of life is based upon the will of the minority
forcibly imposed upon the majority. It relies upon terror and
oppression, a controlled press and radio, fixed elections, and the
suppression of personal freedoms.

I believe that we must assist free peoples to work out their own
110 destinies in their own way.

I believe our help should be primarily through economic and
financial aid which is essential to economic stability and orderly
political progress.

> Reprinted in: Henry Commager, *Documents of American
> History*, 9th edition, (New Jersey: Prentice Hall, 1973) p. 526.

(d) Russia on the Truman Doctrine

In an address containing venomous slander against the socialist

115   countries, Truman in effect raised the question of the USA undertaking the role of world policeman in order to interfere in the affairs of other countries on the side of reaction and counter-revolution, help to strangle the liberation movement in all parts of the world and openly oppose revolution and socialist development.

120   'At the present moment in world history', Truman declared, 'nearly every nation must choose between alternative ways of life. . . . We cannot allow changes in the status quo'.

    The foreign policy programme outlined in the Truman doctrine was from the very beginning clearly anti-Soviet and anti-socialist.

125   On the very next day after Truman's speech, a representative of the French Foreign Ministry told journalists: 'They have adopted a clear-cut stand directed – it is no longer a secret to anyone – against the USSR. . . . Obviously, this marks a new stage in the relations between the USA and the Soviets. It shows that the US Govern-

130   ment desires to gain a footing in the Mediterranean.' The promin-ent US columnist Walter Lippmann did not mince his words, writing: 'We have selected Turkey and Greece not because they are especially in need of relief, not because they are shining examples of democracy . . . but because they are the strategic gateway to the

135   Black Sea and the heart of the Soviet Union'.

    The Soviet Government and press graphically exposed the imperialist character of the Truman Doctrine. *Pravda* wrote that the doctrine signified further interference in the affairs of other countries. The USA's claims to international leadership were

140   growing together with the appetites of the interested American circles. The newspaper pointed out that in the new historical situation the American politicians were ignoring the fact that the old methods of the colonialists and die-hard statesmen were outworn and doomed.

    The USSR sharply denounced the Truman Doctrine also in the

145   UN, stressing that the USA's attempts to dictate its will to other independent countries were incompatible with the principles proc-laimed by the General Assembly in 1946, one of which was that aid to other countries should not be used as a political weapon.

    The USA's aggressive policies in the regions adjoining the Soviet Union and the People's Democracies led to the further unity of these

150   countries, which were vitally interested in safeguarding peace and the sovereign rights of nations against encroachment by the imperialists.

    A History of Soviet Foreign Policy 1945–70, (Moscow: Pro-gress Publishing 1973) pp. 46–7.

Questions

a   In extract (**a**), how had the Cold War come about, according to Stalin?

b   Is the author of extract (**a**) in agreement with the arguments put forward by Stalin?

c What are the major motives behind Soviet foreign policy, according to extract (**b**)?

d How sympathetic towards Russia is the author of extract (**b**)?

e What is the Truman Doctrine (extract (**c**))?

f Is Russia's attack in extract (**d**) a fair commentary on the Truman Doctrine?

★ *g* Using extracts (**a**)–(**d**), and other information known to you, explain why Russia and the West fell out after 1945.

3 East Europe

(a) Russia and Germany

The Soviet people's victory over German fascism opened up a realistic possibility for setting up a system of collective security under which the world would be free of the fear of war. The attainment of this aim necessitated the settlement of one of the most
5 complex international issues, namely, Germany's reorganisation along democratic, peaceful lines and the prevention of a resurgence of a German military potential capable of threatening peace in Europe and the world. This was one of the cardinal objectives of Soviet foreign policy by which the Soviet Government was guided
10 in working out Allied decisions and implementing practical measures in Germany.

The new Germany could not emerge suddenly. It was not a matter of simply recasting state institutions or reshuffling individual leaders in the club of the former ruling elite. Immense work
15 had to be conducted to uproot German militarism and nazism, extirpate their social foundation, remove their exponents from state institutions, the economy and the social sphere, and remould the way of thinking.

Germany had to compensate as much as possible for the destruc-
20 tion and losses she had inflicted on the Soviet Union, Poland, France, Yugoslavia and other countries. The war criminals and those who helped to plan or carry out the nazi programmes that opened the door to brutality and crime had to be made to answer for their deeds. At the same time, the Germans were given the
25 possibility of beginning a new chapter of their history, a chapter free of aggression and war, of attempts to achieve domination over other peoples and countries and violate their interests and rights.

Germany's economy and her system of political power, justice and education had to be overhauled, democratic liberties restored
30 and Germany prepared for peaceful co-operation in international life.

Ibid, p. 78.

(b) Russia and Europe

German doctors informed the world in 1947 that the population of
the western zone of Germany was starving to death. The population was then receiving a daily ration of 800 calories per person per
35   day. The doctors accused the victorious countries of deliberately
destroying the German people by starvation. They wrote in their
memorandum:

'We consider it our duty as German doctors to declare to the
entire world that what is taking place here is the direct opposite of
40   the 'education in the spirit of democracy' which we were promised;
it is, on the contrary, the destruction of the biological basis of
democracy. The spiritual and physical destruction of a great nation
is taking place before our eyes, and no one can escape responsibility
for this unless he does everything in his power to rescue and help.'

45   In reality, as De Castro points out, the allies had no intention of
starving the population of Germany: the low ration levels in the
postwar period of Germany were the natural consequence of the
destructive war and the disintegration of the world's economy
which it produced. It was the fault of the Germans, in other words,
50   that hunger gripped a number of countries including Germany
itself.

German doctors found powerful words and means to appeal to
the consciences of the peoples of the world against the destruction
of a great nation when hunger reached Germany and the German
55   people began to feel privation, although this was nothing compared
to the tortures the Leningraders endured. The same doctors had
uttered not a word of protest against the undisguised efforts of their
compatriots, the officials of fascist Germany, to destroy the peaceful population of Leningrad by starvation.

Goure, *op. cit.*, pp. 126–7.

(c) Russia stands up to the West

60   Its position was that the peace treaties with Nazi Germany's former
allies had to provide for concrete steps that would show that
aggression did not go unpunished, make it difficult to repeat
aggression in the future and prevent any resurgence of fascism that
had engulfed mankind in the horrors of the Second World War. It
65   therefore insisted that the war criminals should receive the punishment they deserved; that the countries which belonged to the
aggressor coalition should compensate for some of the damage they
had inflicted on the countries attacked by them; and that fascism
should be completely uprooted and measures taken to prevent its
70   revival in the former enemy states.

The Soviet Union insisted that the terms of the peace treaties
with Italy, Rumania, Bulgaria, Hungary and Finland should ensure

to these countries the possibility of unhampered and independent
economic development and of establishing friendly relations with
75 all countries. The USSR resolutely opposed the attempts of the
Western powers to deprive the vanquished states of their economic
independence, to subordinate their national economy to foreign
capital.

The USA and Britain were out to turn Hungary, Rumania and
80 Bulgaria into a sphere of domination by US and British monopo-
lies. They counted on utilising the peace treaties for interference in
the affairs of these countries, deposing the people's governments
and restoring the rule of the exploiting classes. The Soviet Government upset these imperialist plans of the Western powers.

85 It wanted the peace won at such a high price to be a lasting one,
making every effort to preserve the close co-operation with its
wartime allies – the USA, Britain and France – and achieve a peace
settlement in close contact with them.

These efforts came into collision with the ambition of the
90 Western powers headed by the USA to dominate the postwar
world, impose their will on the Soviet Union, dictate onerous·
peace terms on the vanquished states, subordinate them to their
influence, interfere in their internal affairs and prevent them from
effectuating far-reaching democratic reforms that would be objec-
95 tionable to Western imperialist circles.

Soviet foreign policy, pp. 130–1.

Questions

a　According to extract (*a*), in what ways did Germany need to be
changed after World War II?
★　b　Why might the Russians be putting forward the ideas expressed
in this extract?
c　How sympathetic towards Germany is the author of extract (*b*)?
d　Why is the West to blame for European rivalries, according to
extract (*c*)?
★　e　Why did Stalin wish to keep a firm control of Eastern Europe?

VIII   The Final Years

Introduction

Stalin's final years were in many ways merely a poor reflection of what had already occurred in the period 1928–1941. World War II had devastated Russia, with much of her industry in ruins and vast projects, barely completed by 1941, being dynamited so that they would not fall into German hands. The solution was another Five Year Plan, and then another, and another after that. Agriculture had also suffered, and not just at the hands of the invader. In an attempt to remain popular in the desperate early days of the war, Stalin had allowed private incentive to supplant collective farming in some areas. The cessation of hostilities in 1945 meant he could return to true communist methods, much to the dismay of those concerned.

The return to strict pre-war controls immediately after the surrender of Germany upset many, used to greater individual scope during the war and having taken Stalin's pretence of a patriotic and communal war at face value. Distrust and suspicion reappeared as well. Anyone tainted by non-communist influences – notably those who had survived German prisoner of war camps, but even Russian peasants who did not evacuate eastwards as the Germans approached – was liable to imprisonment in the infamous gulags. War heroes, like Zhukov, were seen as rivals and rapidly demoted or pushed aside. A new problem emerged. Stalin would not live forever; but nor would such a man ever groom a successor, a potential rival, while he was still around. Suspicion paved the way for renewed purges; the so-called Leningrad Plot of 1949 saw the execution of a number of the leading communists of that city. The Politburo and Central Committee ceased to meet. No-one dared to disagree with Stalin, an increasingly isolated figure. In January 1953 a Doctors' Plot was uncovered, a plot to kill all leading Russian communists. If reminiscent of the murder of Kirov, that precipitated the massive killings of the 1930s, this Plot came to nothing for Stalin died on March 5, 1953 and soon after it was announced that the plot had never existed.

Stalin's colleagues breathed a collective sigh of relief and then paused; they owed everything to Stalin but now he was gone, and in their new-found freedom they were unsure of what to do next.

1 Reconstruction

(a) Industrial production

On the eve of the First Five Year Plan, in 1928, the production of steel was 4.3 million tons; of coal 35.5 million tons; of oil 11.5 million tons; of electric power 1.9 million kilowatts.

At the end of the first Plan, in 1934, production had increased as
5 follows: steel 9.7 million tons; coal 93.9 million tons; oil 24.2 million tons; electric power 6.3 million kilowatts.

By 1940, on the eve of the German invasion of the Soviet Union, production was as follows: steel 18.3 million tons; coal 166 million tons; oil 31 million tons; electric power 11.3 million kilowatts.

10 At the end of the war, in 1945, production had declined as follows: steel 11.2 million tons; coal 149.3 million tons; oil 19.4 million tons; electric power 10.7 million kilowatts. This in spite of the fact that much heavy industry had been shifted East, and that it had absolute priority.

15 In 1946 Stalin gave new target figures. First the country had to be restored, then the economy had to be sharply expanded, to make the Soviet Union, as he said, 'proof against all accidents'. He envisaged a series of at least three Five Year Plans. And his new target figures for 1960, at the earliest, were: steel 60 million tons;
20 coal 500 million tons; oil 60 million tons. This was as far as Stalin's imagination could stretch. The achievement of these targets in fifteen years seemed not only to all outside observers, but also to the Russians and Stalin himself, to mean at least another fifteen years of privation and unrewarding toil for the Soviet people.

25 And when the target was reached, in 1960, Soviet production would still be far behind American production as it was in 1950: steel 90 million tons; coal 700 million tons; oil 250 million tons.

What in fact had happened? In all cases Stalin's 1960 targets have been surpassed: in 1958 the output of steel was only 2 million tons
30 short of the 1960 total; the 1960 total for coal was reached; the 1960 figure for oil was almost doubled – 113 million tons.

      Crankshaw, Edward (1959) *Khrushchev's Russia* (London: Penguin Books) pp. 25–6.

(b) Plans for agriculture

Stalin the terrible had proved himself a great war leader and, in the later years of the war, had seemed closer to his people than ever before. The people, for their part, had proved their loyalty with
35 their own sacrifices, had come to regard Stalin as their own. They expected he would recognise the new spirit which had grown up between ruler and ruled, would ride them with a gentle rein, would put before everything else the easing of their burdens.

But Stalin thought otherwise. Already in 1946, at the great
40 Victory dinner in the Kremlin, he was telling his Marshals that
every nerve must be strained to push through the recovery of the
Soviet economy in preparation for another war. He was setting
production targets for fifteen years ahead which, as things then
looked, were going to stretch the people to the limit in return for
45 minimal rewards. There was to be no let-up at all.

The first Five Year Plan after the war was known as the plan for
National Reconstruction. Everything went into rebuilding and
developing heavy industry and into shifting the centre of industrial
gravity eastwards away from the vulnerable Ukraine. It would
50 have been bad enough without the catastrophic drought in the
summer of 1946. This, it was later officially admitted by Khrushchev, was the worst drought since 1890. It brought large areas of
the Soviet Union to the edge of starvation at the very moment
when Stalin had been promising to abolish food-rationing. But the
55 famine conditions which would have marked such a calamity at any
earlier date in Russian history were avoided by improved distribu-
tion and drastic action at the centre. The Bolsheviks had at least
conquered famine.
     Ibid, p. 166.

(c) Criticism by Khrushchev

I could already see that our output plan wouldn't be fulfilled. I
60 assigned a group of agricultural experts and economists under
Comrade Starenchko to make a realistic calculation of how much
grain we really could produce. They came up with a figure of
somewhere between 100 and 200 million pood. This was very
little. Before the war the Ukraine had produced as much as 500
65 million pood, and the State had already assigned us an output plan
of 400 million pood for 1946. I felt it was best to approach the
problem honestly. I hoped that if I reported the situation to Stalin
candidly and supported my report with facts and figures, he would
believe me. I wanted to do everything in my power to make Stalin
70 understand our position.

I hoped I could prove I was right this time too, and that Stalin
would understand that my request was not 'sabotage'. This term
was always on hand as a justification for the repression and the
extortion of products from the collective farms. In this case I would
75 be trying to convince Stalin that we couldn't supply the agricultural
products we wanted and needed. Our own country needed them,
and Stalin also wanted to send food to the other Socialist countries,
especially Poland and Germany, which couldn't survive without
our help. Stalin was already building up an alliance and fitting
80 himself with the toga of the leader of future military campaigns. He
would be very unhappy to hear that the Ukraine not only couldn't

fulfil its assigned quota for delivery to the State, but in fact needed food from the State to feed its own people.

Khrushchev, *op. cit.*, p. 252.

(d) Stalin and farming

The recovery and progress of agricultural production did not keep
85   pace with the strides made in industry. The keynote of the procurement policy remained as before the war: the compulsive delivery by the collective farms of fixed quotas to the state at very low prices. A combination of penalties and rewards within the farms attempted to provide more incentives to collective farmers to
90   spend greater effort on work on the collective farm. But the main incentive of profit was lacking, and the farmers still obstinately persisted in their attachment to the private plot which yielded proportionately much greater returns on the tolerated free market. To counteract this trend, increases in taxation were decreed on the
95   income farmers derived from their plots and owners of cows, sheep and poultry were further required to deliver quota from their private produce to the state. This policy towards the peasants not only resulted in a very low standard of living on the farms, where the poorer peasants were often near starvation level, but failed to
100   achieve any substantial increase in agricultural production.

While Stalin was alive the evident failure of the agricultural policy was dissembled in confident claims of success and by the suppression of statistics. Thus in his report to the Nineteenth Party Congress, which met in October 1952, Malenkov boldly claimed
105   that agricultural prosperity had been restored after the ravages caused by the war and that the grain problem, in particular, had been solved 'definitely and finally'. After Stalin's death, figures were published which revealed a very different picture. Thus grain production by 1950 was still below a good pre-war year, after
110   adjustment made for the increased area of the USSR. The stocks of cattle presented an even more alarming picture. For cattle as a whole, figures showed that total stocks were even by the beginning of 1953 still well below the total for 1928, before collectivisation had got under way. To see the full significance of these figures, it
115   must be remembered that the population of the USSR had increased by some 25% since 1928.

There can be no doubt that the decisive factor in these differences of opinion on agricultural policy was the view of Stalin, since it is inconceivable that any party member at that date would have
120   ventured to criticise another in public without first being certain that his criticism had Stalin's backing. Nevertheless, the association of particular leaders with a particular view may reasonably be taken as an indication that this was the view for which the leader had canvassed Stalin's support, and therefore represented his own view

125   on policy. When, shortly before his death, Stalin made his own views on the future of agriculture known, it became evident that he was contemplating reducing still further the incentive to peasants to produce.

> Schapiro, Leonard (1963) *The Communist Party of the Soviet Union* (London: Methuen) pp. 518–19.

Questions

a   Trace the production of steel in the period 1928–1960, according to extract (**a**). Do these figures show that Russian industrial development was a success?

b   According to extract (**b**), why did Stalin demand rapid reconstruction after the war?

c   Are the authors of extracts (**a**) and (**b**) supporters of Stalin's Russia?

d   What does extract (**c**) reveal about the relations between Stalin and his subordinates?

★ e   Why, in this extract, might Stalin wish to supply food to Poland just after the war?

f   With reference to extract (**d**), why did farming not make great improvements after 1945?

g   What are the failures in farming and why were they not admitted to, according to this extract?

2 Politics and death

(a) Stalin's daughter

As he got older, my father had begun to feel lonely. He was so isolated from everyone by this time, so elevated, that he seemed to be living in a vacuum. He had not a soul he could talk to. It was the system of which he himself was the prisoner and in which he was
5   stifling from loneliness, emptiness and lack of human companionship.

   I was always horribly embarrassed even by the modest homage paid us when we went to the Bolshoi Theatre in Moscow and at the banquets in honour of my father's seventieth birthday. I was
10   always afraid my father might at any moment say something that would throw water on everyone; I could see his face twitching with annoyance. 'They open their mouths and yell like fools', he would say, in a tone of angry contempt. Did he perceive the hypocrisy that lay behind homage of this sort? I think so, for he
15   was astonishingly sensitive to hypocrisy and was impossible to lie to.

> Allilyeva, Svetlana (1967) *Twenty Letters to a Friend* (London: Hutchinson) p. 63.

(b) A fellow communist

It was incomprehensible how much he had changed in two or three
years. When I had last seen him, in 1945, he was still lively,
quickwitted, and had a pointed sense of humour. But that was
20 during the war, and it had been, it would seem, Stalin's last effort and
limit. Now he laughed at inanities and shallow jokes. On one occasion he not only failed to get the political point of an anecdote I told
him in which he outsmarted Churchill and Roosevelt, but I had the
impression he was offended, in the manner of old men. I perceived
25 an awkward astonishment on the faces of the rest of the party.

In one thing, though, he was still the Stalin of old; stubborn,
sharp, suspicious whenever anyone disagreed with him. He even
cut Molotov, and one could feel the tension between them.
Everyone paid court to him, avoiding any expression of opinion
30 before he expressed his, and then hastening to agree with him.

Djilas, *op. cit.*, p. 153

(c) Stalin's suspicions

In those days anything could have happened to anyone of us.
Everything depended on what Stalin happened to be thinking when
he glanced in your direction. Sometimes he would glare at you and
say, 'Why don't you look me in the eye today? Why are you
35 averting your eyes from mine?' or some such other stupidity.
Without warning he would turn on you with real viciousness. A
reasonable interrogator would not behave with a hardened criminal
the way Stalin behaved with friends who he had invited to eat with
him at his table.
40 Bulganin once described very well the experience we all had to
live with in those days. We were leaving Stalin's after dinner one
evening and he said, 'You come to Stalin's table as a friend, but you
never know if you'll go home by yourself or if you'll be given a
ride – to prison'. Bulganin was fairly drunk at the time, but what he
45 said accurately depicted how precarious our position was from one
day to the next.

Khrushchev, *op. cit.*, p. 277.

(d) A comment on Khrushchev

Khrushchev was later to give lurid accounts of Stalin at this period.
He was, Khrushchev said, 'a profoundly sick man who suffered
from suspiciousness and persecution mania . . .' In his secret speech
50 Khrushchev described how Stalin could look at a man and say,
'Why are your eyes so shifty today?' or 'Why do you turn so much
today and avoid looking me directly in the eyes?' This picture of
Stalin as a half-crazed ogre was an essential part of Khrushchev's

explanation, in 1956 and after, that the terrible abuses of Stalinism
were basically the responsibility of Stalin alone. But however much
he may have exaggerated to this end, it is certain that Khrushchev's
three years in Moscow did involve a further deterioration in his
relations with Stalin and perhaps – though this can only be
speculation – even some painful heart-searching about the course of
Soviet development.

> Frankland, Mark (1966) *Khrushchev*, (London: Penguin)
> p. 81.

Questions

a   In what ways does Stalin's daughter attempt to excuse her
father's behaviour in extract (*a*)?

b   Compare extracts (*b*) and (*c*) on Stalin's character: to what
extent do the two authors appear to fear him?

c   To what extent does extract (*d*) provide an explanation for the
theories put forward by Khrushchev in extract (*c*)?

d   Do the authors of the four extracts (*a*)–(*d*) generally agree on
Stalin's character in his last years?

(e) The Doctors' Plot

A woman doctor named Timashuk claimed that Zhdanov died
because the doctors on the case purposefully administered im-
proper treatment to him, treatment intended to lead to his death.
Naturally, if this had been true, it would have been the most
outrageous villainy. For doctors to destroy life rather than save it is
the worst sort of crime against nature.

If Stalin had been a normal person, he would not have given
Timashuk's letter a second thought. A few such letters always turn
up from people who are pyschologically unbalanced or who are
scheming to get rid of their enemies. But Stalin was more than
receptive to this sort of literature. In fact, I believe this woman
Timashuk herself was a product of Stalinist policies. Stalin had
instilled in the consciousness of us all the suspicion that we were
surrounded by enemies and that we should try to find an unex-
posed traitor or saboteur in everyone. Stalin called this 'vigilance'
and used to say that if a report was ten per cent true, we should
regard the entire report as fact. But how could you find even ten
per cent truth in a letter like Timashuk's?

> Khrushchev, *op. cit.*, p. 306.

(f) An explanation

Three months after the Congress had ended its deliberations, the
press announced the discovery 'some time ago' of a terrorist group

of doctors. These doctors had allegedly confessed to the murder of Zhdanov, and to having plotted to put out of action a number of leading military figures with the object of weakening the defence of the country. The doctors were among the most distinguished medical specialists in the country. Seven out of the nine named were Jews. The announcement further alleged that some of the accused doctors were agents of the American intelligence service, with which they were said to have established contact through an American-sponsored Jewish philanthropic organisation. The openly anti-Jewish character of the allegations was perhaps a novel feature. In other respects the disclosure of the 'conspiracy' bore every resemblance to the accusations that became familiar in the later '30's. The charges had, of course, been invented from beginning to end, and the confessions obtained by torture – this was officially admitted after Stalin's death in an announcement published in the press of 4 April 1953. There can be little serious doubt that the intended 'trial' of the accused doctors would have been the starting point for further accusations, arrests and purges. The extent of the intended purge and its objects are still a matter for conjecture.

Schapiro, *op. cit.*, p. 548.

(g) Stalin's death

The circumstances of Stalin's death are obscure, but Khrushchev gave one vivid (though scarcely complete) account of it to the American diplomat Averill Harriman:

'One Saturday night he invited us all to his dacha in the country for dinner. Stalin was in good humour. It was a gay evening and we all had a good time. Then we went home. On Sunday's Stalin usually telephoned each one of us to discuss business, but that Sunday he did not call, which struck us as odd. He did not come back to town on Monday, and on Monday evening his body-guard called us and said Stalin was ill. All of us – Beria, Malenkov, Bulganin and I – hurried out to the country to see him. He was already unconscious. A blood clot had paralysed an arm, a leg and his tongue. We stayed with him for three days but he remained unconscious. Then for a time he came out of his coma and we went into his room. A nurse was feeding him tea with a spoon. He shook us by the hand and tried to joke with us, smiling feebly and waving his good arm to a picture over his bed of a baby lamb being fed with a spoon by a little girl.

Some time later he died. I wept. After all, we were his pupils and owed him everything. Like Peter the Great, Stalin fought barbarism with barbarism but he was a great man.'

Khrushchev's reaction to Stalin's death was almost certainly as
ambiguous as his description of it. He undoubtedly felt a sense of
loss to the point of feeling lost himself; many thinking people in
65 Russia who were far from being 'Stalinists' felt the same. But the
reverse of this was a sense of liberation.

> Frankland, *op. cit.*, p. 90.

(h) Reasons for his death?

Stalin's death on 5 March 1953 from a haemorrhage of the brain
halted in its initial stages whatever new assault on the party may
have been in contemplation. He was no longer young, and had
70 already been showing some sign of strain at the time of the
Nineteenth Congress. In the absence of firm evidence it is fruitless
to speculate whether his death was wholly due to natural causes. Of
one thing there is no doubt; for many members of the party, both
highly placed and less eminent, the death of the Leader came only
75 just in time.

> Schapiro, *op. cit.*, p. 551.

Questions

a Do the authors of extracts (**e**) and (**f**) believe in the existence of
the Doctors' Plot?

b What was the purpose of the plot, according to extract (**f**)?

c What impression of Khrushchev's feelings for Stalin is given by
extract (**g**)?

d In extract (**h**), why does the author suggest Stalin might not
have died of natural causes?

★ e Using sources (**g**) and (**h**) and other information known to you,
explain how Stalin's death affected Russia.

3 Assessments

(a) The official view

J. V. Stalin is the genius, the leader and teacher of the Party, the
great strategist of Socialist revolution, helmsman of the Soviet
State and captain of armies. His work is extraordinary for its
variety; his energy truly amazing. The range of questions which
5 engage his attention is immense, embracing the most complex
problems of Marxist–Leninist theory and school text-books; problems of Soviet foreign policy and the municipal affairs of the
proletarian capital: the development of the Great Northern Route
and the reclamation of the Colchian marshes, the advancement of
10 Soviet literature and art and the editing of the model rules for

collective farms; and, lastly, the solution of the most intricate problems in the theory and practice of war.

Everyone is familiar with the cogent and invincible force of Stalin's logic, the crystal clarity of his mind, his iron will, his
15 devotion to the Party, his ardent faith in the people, and love for the people. Everybody is familiar with his modesty, his simplicity of manner, his consideration for people, and his merciless severity towards enemies of the people . . . Stalin is the worthy continuer of the cause of Lenin, or, as it is said in the Party: Stalin is the Lenin of
20 today.

> Alexandrov, A. (1949) *Stalin, a short biography* (Moscow)
> p. 146.

(b) A summary of achievements

The Stalin period is characterised by the following features, all of which are closely associated with his name:

(1) The introduction and execution of the Five Year Plans, starting in 1928 and implying largescale industrialisation and the build-
25   ing of a strong army.
(2) The revolutionising of agriculture by enforcing from above the wholescale collectivisation of farms and the liquidation of the kulak.
(3) The introduction of a new constitution of the U.S.S.R.
30 (4) The liquidation in a gigantic purge and in a series of spectacular treason trials of all remaining enemies of the Stalin policy among the old Bolsheviks and the lesser fry of their partisans, in the army, in the civil administration, and in the country as a whole.
35 (5) The prosecution in the field of foreign relations of a consistent and comprehensive peace policy with the simultaneous switch-ing over from the internationally subversive policy of World Revolution of the Comintern to an anti-Fascist policy of a United Front with Leftist parties abroad for the defence of the
40   U.S.S.R., a policy which eventually led to the disbanding of the Comintern.
(6) The endeavour to keep the U.S.S.R. out of the present war by an agreement with Germany, the occupation of a more favour-able defensive position towards Germany by incorporating the
45   Baltic States, Eastern Poland, Bessarabia, and Northern Buko-vina: and after the invasion of Russia by Germany, the adoption of an alliance with Hitler's main enemies, Great Britain and the United States.

The inflexible will, the unwillingness to yield, the realistic
50 statesmanship and high organising abilities are perhaps the leading

characteristics of Stalin. He has grasped the necessities of the country better than people who, like Trotsky, saw the world through doctrinaire spectacles. History has proved that Stalin's maxim of 'Socialism in One Country' was a practical proposition,
55   whereas Trotsky's more ambitious 'Permanent Revolution' was a Utopian idea.

   Fruend, *op. cit.*, pp. 567–8.

(c) Stalin's motives

Comrades! In order not to repeat the errors of the past, the Central Committee has declared itself resolutely against the cult of the individual. We consider that Stalin was excessively extolled.
60   However, in the past Stalin doubtless performed great services to the Party, to the working class, and to the international workers movement.

   This question is complicated by the fact that all this which we have just discussed was done during Stalin's life, under his leader-
65   ship and with his concurrence; here Stalin was convinced that this was necessary for the defence of the working classes against the plotting of enemies and against the attack of the imperialist camp. He saw this from the position of the interest of the working class, of the interest of the labouring people, of the interest of the victory
70   of Socialism and Communism. We cannot say these were the deeds of a giddy despot. He considered that this should be done in the interest of the Party; of the working masses, in the name of the defence of the revolution's gains. In this lies the whole tragedy.

   Khrushchev, *op. cit.*, p. 640.

(d) Stalin and communist development

If we assume the viewpoint of humanity and freedom, history does
75   not know a despot as brutal and cynical as Stalin. He was methodical, all-embracing and total as a criminal. He was one of those rare terrible dogmatists capable of destroying nine-tenths of the human race to make happy the one tenth.

   However, if we wish to determine what Stalin really meant in
80   the history of communism, then he must for the present be regarded as being, next to Lenin, the most grandiose figure. He did not substantially develop the ideas of communism, but he championed them and brought them to realisation in a society and a state. He did not construct an ideal society – something of that sort
85   is not even possible in the very nature of humans and human society, but he transformed backward Russia into an industrial power and an empire that is ever more resolutely and implacably aspiring to world mastery.

Viewed from the standpoint of success and political adroitness,
Stalin is hardly surpassed by any statesman of his time.

All in all, Stalin was a monster who, while adhering to abstract,
absolute, and fundamentally utopian ideas, in practice recognised,
and could recognise, only success – violence, physical and spiritual
extermination.

However, let us not be unjust towards Stalin. What he wished to
accomplish, and even which he did accomplish, could not be
accomplished in any other way.

Djilas, *op. cit.*, p. 190.

Questions

a What were Stalin's greatest achievements, according to extract
   (**a**)?
b What aspects of his career are omitted from this summary?
c Does the author of extract (**b**) approve of Stalin's career overall?
d Compare extracts (**c**) and (**d**): how positive are they towards
   Stalin?
e Compare extracts (**a**)–(**d**) on Stalin's contribution to the development of the communist party.
★ f Why, do you think, none of the extracts (**a**)–(**d**) is totally
   negative towards Stalin?